CONTEMPORARY Smocking

CONTEMPORARY
Smocking

Dorothea Hall

GUILD OF MASTER CRAFTSMAN PUBLICATIONS LTD

First published 1999 by
Guild of Master Craftsman Publications Ltd,
166 High Street, Lewes,
East Sussex BN7 1XU

Reprinted 2000

© Guild of Master Craftsman Publications 1999

ISBN 1 86108 141 3

Photographs by Zul Mukhida
Charts and illustrations by Gail Lawther

Edited by Gail Lawther
Designed by Christopher Lawther
Typefaces: ITC Esprit and Stone Sans

Colour reproduction by Viscan Graphics (Singapore)

Printed and bound in China by Sun Fung Offset Binding Company Limited.

CONTENTS

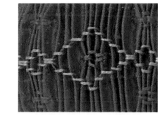

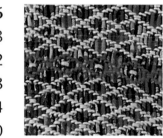

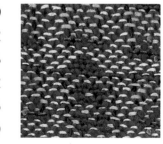

INTRODUCTION

Smocking is one of the prettiest ways of securing gathered fabric; and because it has never really gone out of fashion, most of us are quite familiar with the technique. It's mainly used on garments where elasticity is needed, such as the bodice and sleeves of babies' and children's dresses, but it can also be used as a textured fabric in its own right – adding a touch of style and dash to contemporary items such as cushion covers and mounted pictures.

Traditional designs for an embroidery box from Berkshire, England

In the past, this unique style of embroidery has been used in many countries, evolving as a means of shaping and controlling the fullness of a garment. Smocking uses broad bands of gathering, held in place with rows of stitches worked evenly over the folds. In England, smocking was traditionally worked on land-workers' smocks (or overshirts), to control fullness and yet allow sufficient stretch across the front and back of the garment. The fullness of the sleeves was also shaped by deep bands of smocking at the wrists, which were fastened with three or four Dorset wheel buttons.

The smock can be traced back to medieval times, and was worn by farmers and their labourers, shop-keepers and carters for centuries. The original fabrics would have been home-spun linen, drabbet and spun flax, embroidered with self-coloured linen thread. The basic smock was made up of rectangular pieces of fabric, and many had identical fronts and backs so that they could be worn first one way and then the other to save wear. Although the smock never changed its basic shape, it was adapted to the particular trade of the wearer – a carter, for example, would have a very wide collar and an inside pocket, and it would be quite short to enable him to climb on and off his cart more easily. In contrast a shepherd would wear a longer oiled smock for warmth, and under the full skirt he could also protect young lambs from cold and wet weather.

From a relatively small group of smocking stitches – rope, stem, Vandyke, cable and chevron – a myriad combinations of diamond and wave patterns developed. At the height of its popularity, during the mid-nineteenth century, the two honeycomb stitches and the three feather stitches were included in smocking patterns. It was also usual to include embroidered boxes at each side of the smocked panel, which incorporated regional variations of emblems denoting the wearer's occupation, such as wheels for a carter, crooks and hearts for a shepherd and leaves and trees for a woodsman. Wedding dates and initials were also often lovingly worked into the designs, using single, double and treble feather stitch, stem, chain stitch and french knots, adding individual character to each garment. These boxes were embroidered to strengthen the places most likely to wear. In some cases, the shoulders of the smock were embroidered with emblems, or gathered and embroidered epaulettes were added to give the wearer extra protection against rain and the rubbing of yokes. Eventually, as the surface embroidery became more elaborate, the 'best' smock had become such a special garment it was worn with pride on many social occasions such as weddings and funerals.

The beauty of a piece of smocking relies on the way in which the stitching shapes the gathered fabric into decorative units. The juxtaposition of the surrounding unstitched gathers, the elasticity and the play of light and shadow are as important as the surface textures and the patterns of the smocking stitches themselves. The simple country smock has been the inspiration for countless people who, over the years, have smocked babies' and children's clothes – on plain and patterned fabrics, in matching and contrasting colours – and have kept alive this intriguing form of embroidery. More recently, textile artists have explored manipulating the surfaces of fabrics as a means of artistic expression – gathering the surfaces evenly and unevenly to create

Traditional designs for embroidered boxes from Lancashire, England

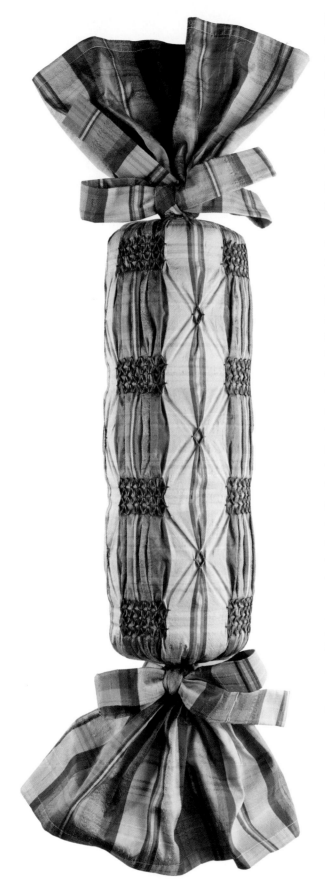

interesting shadows and three-dimensional effects. They may use their own interpretations of conventional smocking stitches to secure the folds or any other means, including machine stitching – perhaps stitching regularly or randomly across the folds to create ripple effects, turning the folds first one way and then the other. With experimentation in mind, the permutations and possibilities are endless.

If you are new to smocking, you will quickly realize that a few simple ground rules should be learned first; then, when you've achieved a measure of confidence in the technique, you can try a more experimental approach, perhaps breaking some of the rules – bear in mind, though, that the simplest ideas are often the most effective and enduring. You will see from the projects in the book that not all smocking is necessarily worked the traditional way of creating solid bands of stitching over a grid of dots; it can also be worked in small 'spot' areas using the woven plaid or checked fabric as the grid – see the tartan bolster on page 52. Working directly onto the fabric in this way, you can smock as much or as little as you like, using regular repeats or covering the area in an all-over random way. If, for example, you were honeycomb stitching a checked fabric such as the laundry bag on page 44, the woven checks (or grid) could be as big as 2–3cm ($3/4–1^1/4$in). This means that the smocking progresses really quickly. Full-size curtain headings can be worked like this but, for fabrics other than checks or coarse fabrics where the threads can be counted, you would have to mark out the grid with a ruler and pencil, also marking in the dots.

As a textile artist, I'm always aware of the tactile qualities of fabrics, threads and embellishments, and how important it is when designing to make the right choice to express a personal statement. Smocking lends itself very well to having buttons and beads, cords and tassels incorporated into the design, and if this is done tastefully it needn't look at all overworked or complicated. Beads for example, especially small glass beads, have a special tactile quality; you will notice as they are stitched into all-over designs that a certain magic occurs. Combined with the light and shadow already created by the smocking, the beaded surface begins to twinkle, adding highlights and a surprising coldness to the touch. The beads also add a weight and fluidity to the smocking that wasn't there before – the finished fabric seems to have a completely different structure. We know that discretion and balance coupled with originality are some of the essential elements in good design, but I would also include the sense of touch as a delightful bonus.

In designing the projects for the book, I've taken traditional smocking techniques and stitches as a starting point and used them in a variety of easy-to-make items

that I think will appeal to most people. In other slightly more complicated projects, such as the nine-patch cushion on page 80, I've shown, in fairly vibrant colours, how embroidered motifs can complement simple smocking stitches to great effect. Conversely, the girl's bag on page 74 emphasizes deep surface texture and line embroidery, with its subtle ground fabric tightly gathered to resemble woven grass and then stitched with geometric patterns. In the house and garden picture on page 110, by using smocking as a textured fabric I've tried to liberate the style of smocking design and demonstrate that other images are possible – and, as always, original ideas can be great fun to create.

Whether you are a beginner or a more experienced embroiderer, I hope you will enjoy making these projects as much as I have, and that with a little practice, the techniques and ideas given here can provide the stimulus and inspiration to develop your own potential and creative approach to smocking.

SMOCKING TECHNIQUES

The basic techniques and methods for working smocking, whether it's a child's garment or a sofa cushion, are very much the same. It's important, though, to fully understand the various techniques described in the following pages, and to be able to use them confidently, before starting the projects given in the book. I've always found that the quickest way to learn a new discipline is to carry out the instructions as you read them, working on a spare piece of fabric – in other words, practising as you go. Then you can always cross-refer to your samples if you get stuck at any stage of a project later on.

Fine/medium-weight fabrics suitable for smocking, including cotton lawn, patterned lawn and cotton piqué

Fabric

Almost any fabric that will gather easily is suitable for smocking. For children's wear, fine to medium fabrics are best; these include plain and patterned cotton, lawn, cotton piqué, chambray, gingham, voile, batiste, fine silks and linens. For decorative home furnishings, such as cushion covers and curtain headings, heavier linens and silks should be used.

The width of fabric required for smocking depends on the type being used (light or heavyweight), the distance between the folds and the tension of the stitches. As a general rule, three times the width of the finished item should be allowed, bearing in mind that thicker fabrics usually require a little less and finer fabrics a little more. A scented drawer sachet, for example, measuring 10cm (4in) across, requires a width of 30cm (12in) for the gathering, plus seam allowances for the sides.

The fabric is gathered by working rows of running stitches across it on the wrong side, drawing the threads up into even gathers and tying them securely. To help ensure that the gathered folds are even, the points to be picked up on the fabric are usually marked with the help of iron-on transfer dots. In addition to the transfer method, smocking can be worked on other fabrics which have their own built-in 'grid', such as dotted and checked patterns; and also on heavier fabrics that have a pronounced weave, where the threads can be counted evenly.

Working on the right side of the gathers, bands or all-over patterns of decorative smocking stitches are grouped according to the amount of elasticity required. Areas of gathered fabric can also be left unsmocked and later embroidered with decorative stitching and motifs. Always work the smocking before assembling the item.

Threads

Most embroidery threads can be used successfully in smocking, but it is important to choose a thread which suits the weight of the fabric being used, and which gives the right balance between the stitching and the gathered folds.

Single threads, such as coton à broder, linen thread, twisted pearl, metallics and stranded embroidery threads, can all be used. Six-stranded silk and cotton threads are popular because they can easily be divided into different multiples of strands for working different weights of fabric.

For best results, the thread should not be too thick, but should slide easily through the fabric. Neither should it be too thin, or too pale in colour so that it can't be seen. After all, the prettiness of smocking depends on being able to see well-defined stitching and the variety of patterns the stitches make on the gathered folds.

For smocking patterned fabrics, use stronger than normal colours so that they will show up clearly. Often in printed fabrics there are one or two accent colours that can be picked out and complemented with the smocking threads.

Fabrics such as these, which have strong spot or check patterns, can be combined very effectively with smocking, using their 'built-in' grids to help position the stitches

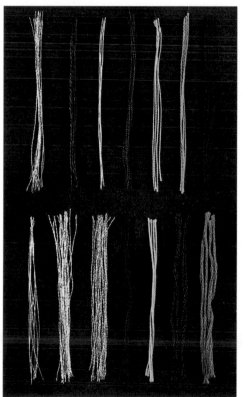

A selection of threads suitable for working the smocking stitches, including stranded cotton, coton à broder, pearl cotton, flower thread, and single and stranded metallic threads

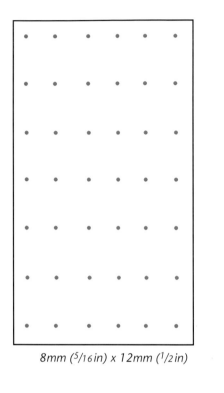

8mm (5/16in) x 12mm (1/2in)

Transfer dots

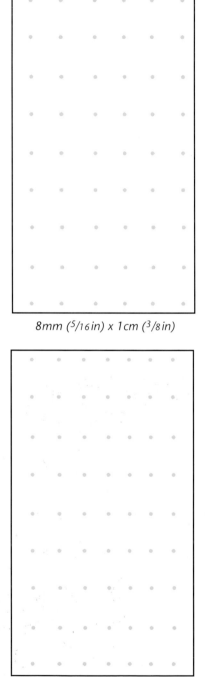

8mm (5/16in) x 1cm (3/8in)

6mm (1/4in) x 1cm (3/8in)

Needles

Crewel needles in sizes 5 to 7 will suit most fabrics (7 being the smallest).

Transfer dots

Transfer dots are available in most needlework stores, and are sold as separate sheets measuring 114cm (45in) wide by 20cm (8in) deep. There are various spacings between the dots, but the most popular sizes are 8mm (5/16in) across by 12mm (1/2in) down, and 6mm (1/4in) across by 1cm (3/8in) down – the smallest spacing is used for finer fabrics and vice versa. Most transfer dots are either silver or pale blue, which seems to suit both dark- and light-coloured fabrics; silver tends to produce a darker dot, more suitable for light colours, while pale blue dots show up well on darker shades.

The dots are printed in even rows, which makes it easy to cut the paper to size – cutting in between the rows. For deeper areas of smocking, you can join two or more lengths of transfer paper by butting up the edges and securing them with short strips of sticky tape. Small left-over pieces can also be joined in this way, so that nothing is wasted.

Two impressions

Sometimes it's possible to use a transfer twice, particularly if a very light touch from the iron was used the first time around. If, for example, you've used only light pressure on medium-weight cotton or silk, keep the transfer and try using it a second time on finer fabrics, such as sheers or muslin, using a slightly heavier pressure. If any dots are unclear, proceed as for semi-transparent fabrics below.

Semi-transparent fabrics

Old transfers can also be used with semi-transparent fabrics by placing them underneath the fabric and marking the rows of dots with an H pencil, as in the lavender sachet on page 21. This is obviously better for smaller rather than larger smocking projects, but not impossible to use for either.

Transferring the dots

Begin by pressing the fabric to remove all creases, and place it right side down on the ironing board. Mark the area to be gathered with pins. Cut out the smocking dots to size and position them on the fabric, ink side down, inside the seam allowances. Pin the paper to the fabric, carefully placing a minimum number of pins at each side between the rows of dots. (For covering larger areas, join the transfer paper evenly and secure with sticky tape.) Pass a medium-hot iron lightly over the dots (right), working with a lifting action. Remove the paper as you press; this reminds you not to over-press the transfer, which may slip, and also to prevent the dots from becoming too dark and showing on the right side.

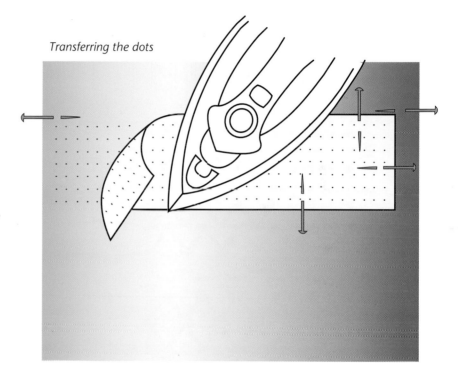

Transferring the dots

Gathering the fabric

Using a length of strong sewing thread, measured across the width of one row plus a little extra for tying, begin with a large knot and work running stitches across the row. Working from right to left, pick up a small amount of fabric under each dot and, at the end of the row, unthread the needle and leave the thread loose (right). Complete all the rows in the same way. (If you are left-handed, work in the same way but from left to right.)

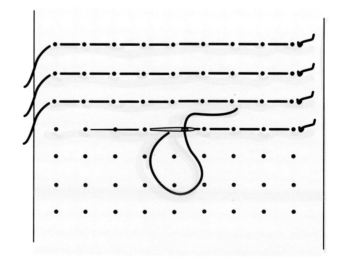

Gathering the fabric

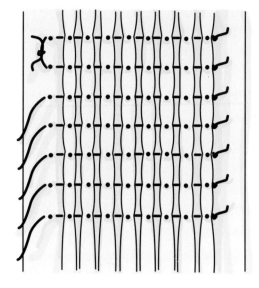

Preparing the folds

Work with one pair of threads at a time and pull them up evenly, gently easing the fabric along the length of the threads. Complete all the rows, pulling the threads tightly at first to crease the folds and then releasing them to the required width. When calculating the required width, remember that the smocking will always relax a little when the gathering threads are removed. Tie the threads securely in pairs (left), close to the last fold. Even out the gathers by gently stroking between each fold with a needle.

Working the smocking from a chart

Every chart shows the smocking pattern drawn with simplified stitches in colour: sometimes the whole pattern is given, and sometimes a repeat section; each row is also indicated, numbered and annotated with the particular stitch to be worked Every chart has a key which gives the type and colour of thread used. The sample chart (left) shows all these features.

Before you start working on any of the projects, read through the instructions and the chart to check that you understand how the stitching is done, and cross check your work with the chart periodically as your smocking progresses.

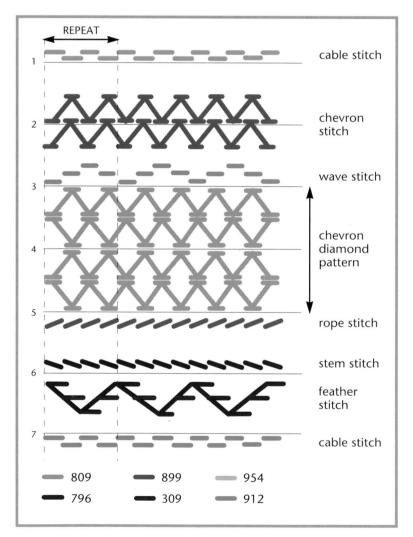

Beginning the smocking

Most stitches are worked from left to right on the right side of the fabric, using the gathering threads as a guide to keeping the rows of stitches straight. Some patterns may position the stitches halfway between rows, just below or just above the gathering threads, but they should still be used to guide straight stitching.

Begin by making a knot at the end of the thread and bring the needle up close to the first fold on the left. Continue stitching, picking up a small amount of fabric at the top of the fold (see above right) as instructed in the stitch diagram. At the end of a row, fasten off the thread on the wrong side by working two small back stitches into the last fold.

You will find diagrams showing you how to work the different stitches at the back of the book. (Once again, if you are left-handed you will need to work the stitches in the opposite direction, so most of them will be worked from right to left. As the stitch diagrams show the needle and working thread for right-handed people, you may find it useful to place a hand-mirror next to the diagram – or prop the book up in front of a mirror and follow the reversed images.)

Pressing

If your finished smocking is the correct size before the gathering threads are removed, then it can be steam pressed on the wrong side (right) before progressing to the making-up stage. If you wish to stretch your smocking slightly to size, or to curve an edge, then remove the gathering threads and pin it to the required size and shape, carefully inserting the pins into the seam allowances only; lightly steam press on the wrong side, so that the folds stay crisp and are not flattened.

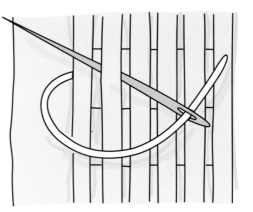

Beginning the smocking

Pressing the smocking lightly on the wrong side

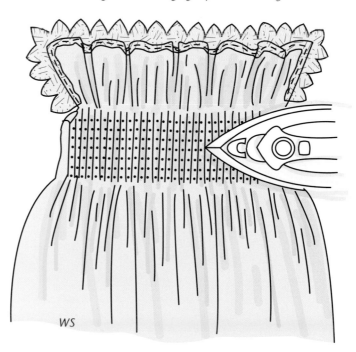

WS

1
Easy projects

Sweet smelling
sachets

◆ ◆ ◆

Scented sleep pillow

◆ ◆ ◆

Bridesmaid's
confetti flute

◆ ◆ ◆

Christmas hanging
bauble

SWEET SMELLING SACHETS

There is nothing quite like the wonderful sensation of wearing freshly perfumed garments or sleeping between delicately scented sheets.

These little sachets, specially made from loosely woven fabrics (so that the scent can easily pass through), and filled with different sweet-smelling flowers and leaves, can be hung inside wardrobes and linen cupboards where they will impart their unique fragrance for many, many months.

SACHET 1   ROSEBUDS

SIZE:
15cm x 12cm (6in x 4³/₄in) minus the hanging loop

THREADS
DMC stranded embroidery cotton: one skein each of pinks 3804, 3607; greens 580, 733

MATERIALS
- 50cm x 20cm (20in x 8in) of white muslin
- Sewing thread to match the fabric
- 50cm (20in) of pre-gathered lace, 1.5cm (⁵/₈in) wide
- Crewel needle, size 7
- One sheet of light-coloured smocking dots, 8mm x 1cm (⁵/₁₆in x ³/₈in)
- 1m (40in) of pink taffeta ribbon, 1.5cm (⁵/₈in) wide
- Scented rosebuds

The frill

1 From one long edge of the muslin, cut a 4.5cm (1³/₄in) strip for the frill facing. Pin the lace to the top edge of the main fabric, right sides together and straight edges even. Place the facing on top right side down (see left); pin, tack and machine stitch along the edge.

2 Turn the facing to the wrong side, press the seam and machine stitch close to the edge on the right side. Tack the facing 2cm (³/₄in) from the edge to secure it while you work.

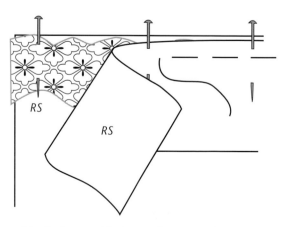

Pin the lace and facing to the main fabric

The smocking

3 Cut out 13 rows of dots to the width of the muslin and transfer them to the wrong side of the fabric, placing the top row just over the edge of the facing and leaving 1cm ($^3/_8$in) seam allowances at each side. Gather the rows of dots, using a long length of sewing thread for each row. Pull up the gathers tightly to set the folds and then release them to measure 16.5cm ($6^1/_2$in) at the top edge and 19cm ($7^1/_2$in) at the bottom; knot the threads firmly in pairs.

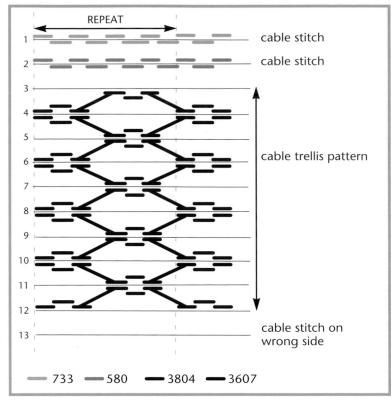

REPEAT

1   cable stitch

2   cable stitch

3

4

5

6   cable trellis pattern

7

8

9

10

11

12

13   cable stitch on wrong side

— 733   — 580   — 3804   — 3607

Rosebuds smocking chart

4 Following the smocking chart given left, begin with the top two rows of cable stitch using two strands of thread in the needle. (See page 118 onwards for how to work the stitches.) Keep the tension fairly loose for the whole design, and work the main part in alternate rows of pink to create the pretty cable trellis pattern.

On the wrong side, work the bottom row of cable stitch in sewing thread.

5 Remove the gathering threads. Place the smocking face down on your ironing board, pin to shape and lightly steam press. With right sides together and patterns matching, pin and stitch the side seam. Press the seam open and position it at the centre back, overcasting it at the frill to neaten it.

6 Pin the bottom edges together and stitch a seam through the cable stitching; trim the corners and turn through to the right side.

Ribbon ties

7 Cut 28cm (11in) of pink ribbon for the loop, and hand stitch the ends inside the frill at the centre back and at the front.

8 Fill the sachet with rosebuds. Gather the top through the rows of cable stitching and then tie the remaining ribbon around, finishing with a floppy bow.

For a special gift, attach one or two rosebuds to the bow.

SACHET 2 — LAVENDER

SIZE:
30cm x 15cm (12in x 6in) minus the hanging loop

THREADS
DMC stranded embroidery cotton: one skein each of lavender 340; green 958; deep pink 3804

MATERIALS
- ➤ 42cm x 34cm (16½in x 13½in) of white organdie
- ➤ Sewing thread to match the fabric
- ➤ Light-coloured smocking dots: 6mm x 1cm (¼in x ⅜in)
- ➤ 1m (40in) of lavender taffeta ribbon, 1.5cm (⅝in) wide
- ➤ 50cm (20in) of deep pink silk ribbon, 6mm (¼in) wide
- ➤ Crewel needle, size 7
- ➤ Sprigs of lavender

The frill

1 To make the frill, fold 10cm (4in) to the wrong side on one short edge of the organdie. Press, then tack across the top and bottom edges of the frill and across the centre to secure the layers.

The smocking

2 Cut out five rows of dots to the width of the organdie and apply to the wrong side, aligning the bottom row with the raw edge of the frill. Stitching through both layers, gather the dots, using a long length of sewing thread for each row. Pull up the threads in pairs, tightly at first to crease the folds and then releasing them to measure 13cm (5in) across the top row and 15cm (6in) across the bottom. Knot firmly.

3 Follow the smocking chart given on page 22 and, with two strands of thread in the needle, work the two rows of rope and stem stitch first, to stabilize the folds. Then work the centre rows of Vandyke stitch, and finish with the top and bottom rows of cable stitch. (See page 118 onwards for how to work the stitches.) Remove the gathering threads and the tacking stitches.

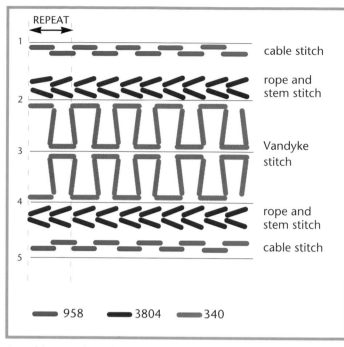

REPEAT

1   cable stitch

2   rope and stem stitch

3   Vandyke stitch

4   rope and stem stitch

5   cable stitch

958   3804   340

Lavender smocking chart

Making the sachet

4 Fold the lavender ribbon in half and, with the right sides facing, pin the folded edge inside the seam allowance, level with the smocking. With right sides together, pin and stitch the side and bottom edges, catching the ribbon in the seam. Turn through to the right side. Fold the ribbon for the hanging loop in half and hand stitch inside the frill, close to the top row of smocking.

5 Insert the lavender, leaving just the ends of the stems protruding. Close the top with one or two french knots worked in red across the centre of the smocking, on both sides. After working the first knot, take the thread through to the other side, work the second knot and then slip the needle between the layers and bring it out ready to make the next pair of knots.

6 To finish, tie the ribbon into a bow with long floaty tails.

SACHET 3

SIZE:
15cm x 12cm (6in x 4³/₄in) minus the hanging loop

THREADS
DMC stranded embroidery cotton: one skein each of pinks 961, 3326; yellows 725, 727, 3820; blue 3766; green 907

POT POURRI

MATERIALS
➤ Two pieces of unbleached calico, 23cm x 23cm (9in x 9in)
➤ 76cm (30in) of cream lace, 2cm (³/₄in) wide
➤ 1m (40in) of cream ribbon, 6mm (¹/₄in) wide
➤ Light-coloured smocking dots, 6mm x 1cm (¹/₄in x ³/₈in)
➤ Crewel needle, size 7
➤ One decorative pearl button, 12mm (¹/₂in) diameter
➤ Four small pearl buttons, 6mm (¹/₄in) diameter
➤ Tracing paper, dressmaker's carbon paper

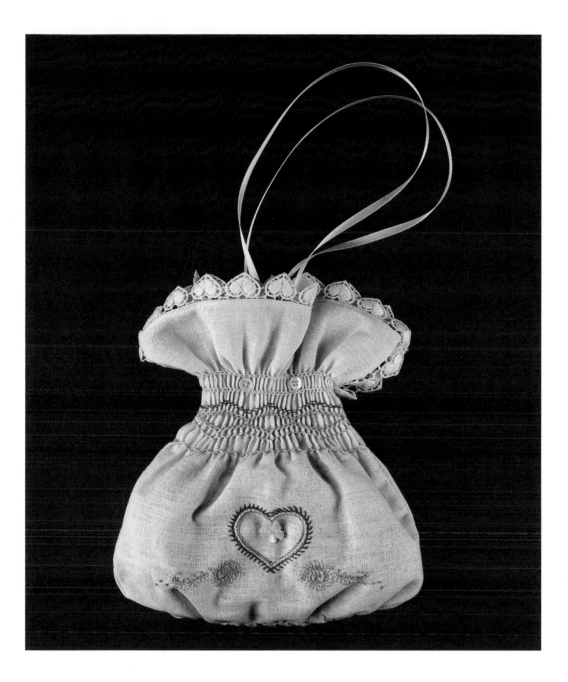

The heart and scroll embroidery (optional)

1 Transfer the motifs (see page 25) to the right side of the sachet front using the carbon paper method (see page 137). Using two strands of embroidery thread in the needle, work the heart and scroll motifs in stem and feather stitch, as shown, finishing the scrolls with french knots. Stitch the button to the centre heart using yellow 3820 embroidery thread.

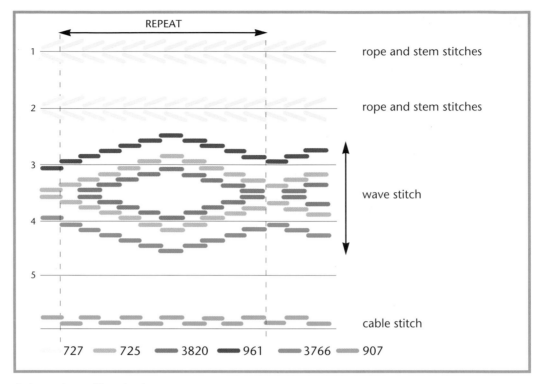

1   rope and stem stitches

2   rope and stem stitches

3   wave stitch

4

5

cable stitch

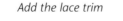 727   725   3820   961   3766   907

Pot pourri smocking chart

Add the lace trim

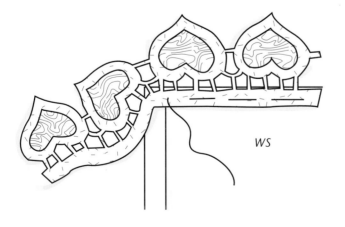

WS

The smocking

2 Cut out two sets of 6 rows of dots and position one set on the wrong side of each piece of calico, placing the top row 5cm (2in) below the top edge. Pin in place and lightly press with a warm iron. Gather the dots and pull the threads up in pairs, tightly at first and then releasing them to measure 7.5cm (3in) across the top and 10cm (4in) at the bottom. Knot the ends firmly and even out the gathers.

3 Following the smocking chart above and working with an even tension, begin with the top two rows of rope and stem stitch, using two strands of embroidery cotton in the needle. (See page 118 onwards for how to work the stitches.) Complete the centre band of wave stitch, and then the bottom row of cable stitch with a loose tension.

4 Repeat the smocking on the second piece of calico. Remove the gathering threads, then pin out the smocking to shape, wrong side down on your ironing board, and lightly steam press.

The lace trim

5 On the top edge of both front and back sections, make narrow single turnings to the wrong side; continue the turnings down the sides as far as the smocking. Pin and tack the lace in place, covering the raw edges (see bottom left), then machine stitch from the right side.

The hanging loops

6 Cut the ribbon in half. Fold each length in half again and hand stitch the raw edges to the wrong side of the smocking, at the centre front and back.

7 Machine stitch a gathering thread along the bottom edge of both pieces; pull up by about 2.5cm (1in) and knot.

Making the sachet

8 With the back and front sections right sides together and the rows of smocking even, pin, tack and machine stitch around the sachet, starting and finishing just below the top rows of smocking. Take 12mm ($^{1}/_{2}$in) seams all round, and slightly curve the lower corners. Trim the corners and turn the sachet through to the right side. Fill with pot pourri, and either knot the hanging loops together to close the opening or stitch the four pearl buttons in pairs to each side of the sachet, inside the top border.

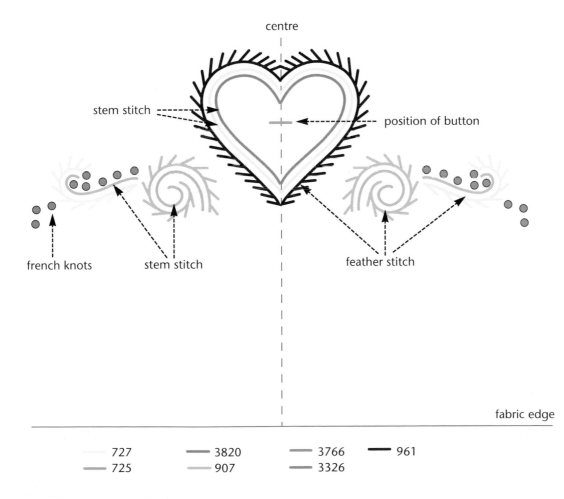

centre

stem stitch

position of button

french knots   stem stitch

feather stitch

fabric edge

727   3820   3766   961
725   907   3326

Pot pourri embroidery motif

SCENTED SLEEP PILLOW

A pretty pillow of pure silk, embroidered in pinks and greens and filled with fragrant flower petals, makes a delightful feminine present, and a comforting, sleep-inducing headrest.

Dried flower fillings, such as lavender and roses, are stitched in a muslin sachet before being placed inside the pillow cover. To prevent dried petals from becoming crackly, and so interrupting slumber, simply add a few drops of lavender or rose oil to the mixture before you fill the sachet.

In this design, clever use is made of the gathered fabric at each end of the smocking to create the side frills; the pillow cover itself is neatly zipped at the back so that it can easily be removed for cleaning.

SIZE

28cm x 16.5cm
(11in x 6½in)

THREADS

DMC stranded embroidery cotton: one skein each of pinks 776, 961; green 3031

MATERIALS

➤ Pink dupion silk:
56cm x 33cm (22½in x 13in) for the pillow front;
23cm x 20cm (9in x 8in) for the pillow back
➤ 15cm (6in) matching fine zip
➤ Sewing silk to match the fabric
➤ One sheet of smocking dots: 8mm x 1cm (⁵/₁₆in x ³/₈in)
➤ Crewel needle, size 7
➤ Two pieces of muslin, 15cm x 13cm (6in x 5in)
➤ Lavender or scented rose petals

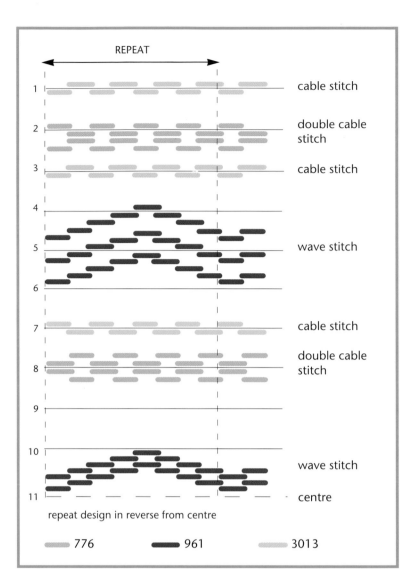

1	cable stitch
2	double cable stitch
3	cable stitch
4	
5	wave stitch
6	
7	cable stitch
8	double cable stitch
9	
10	wave stitch
11	centre

repeat design in reverse from centre

776   961   3013

Preparing the fabric

1 Cut out 21 rows of dots, butting together and securing two sections of transfer paper if necessary. Apply them centrally to the wrong side of the pillow front, leaving 6.5cm (2½in) at the top and bottom for the frill, and 1.5cm (⅝in) seam allowance along the side edges.

Neatening the frill

2 To neaten the raw edges of the frill, press 6mm (¼in) double turnings to the wrong side of the long edges, and then down the side edges for about 3cm (1¼in). Pin to hold. Using matching silk sewing thread, finish the hem with shell hemming stitch (see page 134 for how to work the stitch).

The smocking

3 Working with long lengths of thread to span the width of the fabric, pick up the rows of dots using running stitch. Working with the threads in pairs, pull them up very tightly to set the fabric folds (the last row can be pulled up and knotted together with the previous pair). Release the gathers so that they measure 18cm (7in) across.

4 Using three stands of embroidery cotton in the needle and following the smocking chart given above left, work the first half of the design from the top to the centre line as marked. Then turn the chart upside down and repeat the smocking to complete the other half of the design. (See page 118 onwards for instructions on how to work the stitches.)

Because of the nature of slub silk, you may find that you need to take extra care to form your stitches evenly.

5 Except for the top and bottom rows, remove the gathering threads and, if necessary, lightly press the work to size on the wrong side.

The zip closure

6 Cut the back section of silk in half to give two pieces measuring 20cm x 11.5cm (8in x 4$\frac{1}{2}$in). Following the instructions on page 135, join the centre seam at each end and insert the zip.

7 With the zip closed and the back and front sections right sides together, pin and machine stitch the two side seams. Turn through to the right side. At the back, fold in the top and bottom seam allowances, then pin and tack the layers together (see top right). Working from the front, machine stitch just below the top row of cable stitch, using a fairly long stitch.

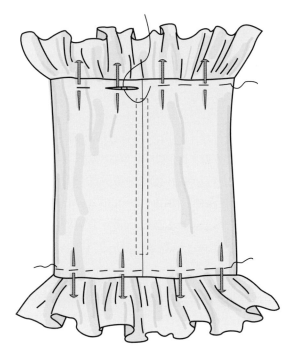

Tack the top and bottom seams

Making the inner sachet

8 Pin the two pieces of muslin together and machine zigzag stitch around three sides. Fill (not too generously) with lavender or scented rose petals. Close the opening with zigzag stitch, and insert the muslin sachet into the pillow cover. To revive the original perfume, simply sprinkle a few drops of essential oil onto the inner sachet.

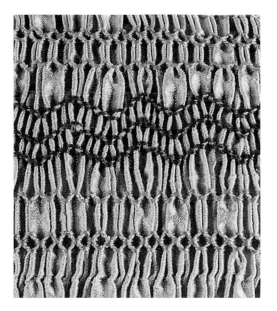

BRIDESMAID'S CONFETTI FLUTE

I've always liked the idea that the container in which a bridesmaid carries her confetti should be given to her as a special keepsake from the wedding day.

This little 'flute' seemed to make its own shape as I tried to retain the fabric fullness for the integral frill at the top and yet gather in the bottom edge. Aiming at a Fabergé effect, the smocking is worked on a pure silk ground entirely in gold thread, which lends a contrasting lustre to the pearls and gold bead decoration on the frill.

The flute is softly lined, to prevent confetti from getting inside the gathers, and its long ribbon loops can either be knotted together or used to hang the flute from the bridesmaid's wrist.

SIZE
16cm (6$^{1}/_{2}$in) long, 38cm (15in) around frill, 4cm (1$^{1}/_{2}$in) across lower edge

THREADS
DMC light gold metallic thread, one reel

MATERIALS
➤ 48cm x 24cm (19in x 9$^{1}/_{2}$in) of ivory dupion silk (with selvedge on the long edge)
➤ 25cm x 25cm (10in x 10in) of contrast cotton lawn or fine silk for the lining
➤ One sheet of smocking dots: 8mm x 1cm ($^{5}/_{16}$in x $^{3}/_{8}$in)
➤ Silk sewing thread to match the fabric
➤ Crewel needles, sizes 7 and 9
➤ 20 pearl beads, 3mm ($^{1}/_{8}$in) diameter
➤ DMC gold metallic beads 08729, one box
➤ 1m (40in) of ivory silk ribbon, 6mm ($^{1}/_{4}$in) wide

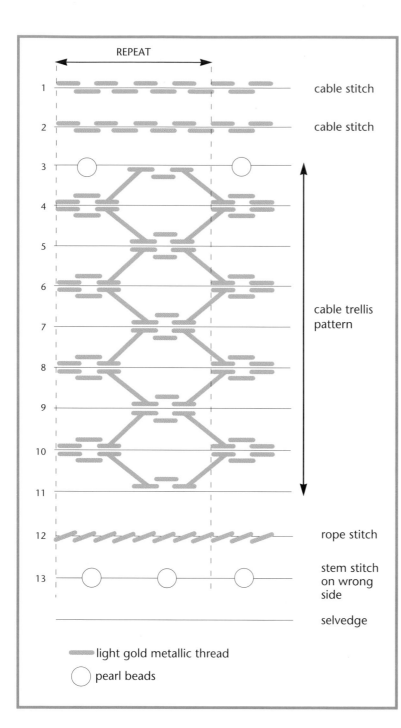

1	cable stitch
2	cable stitch
3	
4	
5	
6	cable trellis pattern
7	
8	
9	
10	
11	
12	rope stitch
13	stem stitch on wrong side
	selvedge

REPEAT

▬▬ light gold metallic thread

◯ pearl beads

Preparing the fabric

1 Lightly press the silk on the wrong side to remove any creases. Cut out the rectangle for the confetti holder to measure 48cm x 18cm (19in x 7in) with the selvedge running along one long side; this leaves a narrow rectangle 48cm x 6cm (19in x 2½in) for the frill facing.

2 With right sides together and the selvedge at the bottom, pin and machine stitch the frill facing to the top edge. Press and turn to the wrong side. Overcast the raw short edges to prevent them from fraying.

Decorating the frill

3 Using ivory silk sewing thread, apply single gold beads to the top edge of the frill, spacing them at 8mm (5/16in) intervals, and leaving 12mm (½in) seam allowances at each side. (See page 129 for how to apply beads.) Then apply more gold beads, 6mm (¼in) below the edge but in every other space made by the first row, stitching a bead to both sides of the frill.

After stitching on the second bead of each pair, slip the needle between the fabric to emerge at the next position, ready for the next pair.

The smocking

4 From the sheet of dots, cut out 13 rows and pin them to the wrong side of the fabric, placing the top two rows over the lower edge of the facing. Working in this way through double fabric helps to keep the fluted shape. Press with a warm dry iron to transfer the dots.

Gather the dots, using long lengths of thread, and pull the rows up tightly. Release the gathers so that the fabric (including the seam allowances) measures 20cm (8in) across the top row and 11.5cm (4½in) across the bottom row.

5 Using gold thread in the needle and following the smocking chart given on page 32, work the trellis pattern, beginning with an even tension and then gradually tightening the tension towards the bottom. (See page 118 onwards for how to work the stitches.) On rows 1 and 2 work the cable stitch with a relaxed tension. On row 12, work the rope stitch very firmly. Finally, using silk sewing thread, work row 13 on the wrong side pulling the stem stitch as firmly as possible to draw in the shape. Remove the gathering threads.

6 Place the smocking right side down on your ironing board and pin out to measure 23cm (9in) across the top of the smocking and 11.5cm (4½in) across the bottom. Lightly press with a dry medium iron, avoiding pressing the frill.

7 Following the smocking chart and using silk sewing thread, apply the pearl beads to the top edge of the diamond pattern as shown.

Making the confetti flute

8 At this stage, cut out the lining. Using the smocking as a template, pin it to the lining fabric and cut out, being careful not to snip the frill. Trim 2.5cm (1in) from the top edge of the lining.

9 Begin seaming the smocked fabric by first joining the frill with a narrow french seam. With the frill wrong sides together, pin and stitch a narrow seam finishing just below the two rows of cable stitch. Turn to the wrong side and repeat. Press to one side. Then, with the right sides together, pin and stitch the remainder of the seam. Finger press open and place the seam to the centre back.

10 With right sides together, pin and stitch the side edges of the lining section and press the seam open. On the top edge, make a 12mm (½in) turning and press.

11 Now attach the ribbon loops. Cut the ribbon into two equal lengths; fold each length in half and position them opposite each other, inside the flute, pinning them to the top two rows of smocking (see below). Hand stitch in place.

12 With wrong sides together, slip the lining over the main flute and pin it in place, covering the top two rows of smocking. Using silk sewing thread, neatly hem around the top edge of the lining, gently easing the fullness to fit the elasticity of the smocking, and catching the inner folds only of the gathers.

13 Turn the flute to the right side, smooth the lining inside, and trim the lower edge of the lining if necessary. Close the bottom edge by sewing pearl beads across the width. Attach five to each side, as shown on the chart, slipping the needle between the two layers and bringing it out in the next position, as you did for the gold beads on the frill.

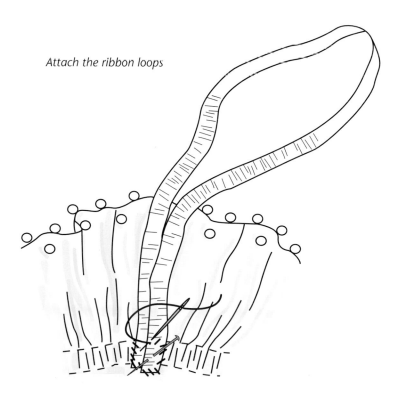

Attach the ribbon loops

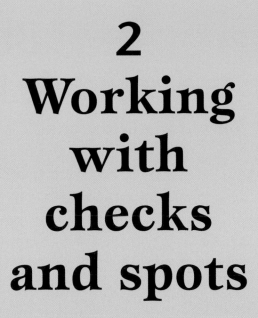

2
Working with checks and spots

Blue and white check cushion

◆ ◆ ◆

Laundry bag

◆ ◆ ◆

Damask spot cushion

◆ ◆ ◆

Tartan bolster

BLUE AND WHITE CHECK CUSHION

Relaxing into inviting cushions on beds, chairs and sofas around the home is a simple luxury we almost take for granted. Cushion shapes and sizes are enormously versatile, and you can select different styles, colours and fabrics to give individuality to the decor of different rooms.

This cushion uses simple gingham checks for working the smocking where, instead of using transfer dots, the corners of the checks are picked up to form the stitch, and the fabric is 'gathered' as you go. The centre panel is worked in Vandyke stitch (in alternate rows of pale blue and green) to create a highly textured surface. Feather stitch is worked on the surrounding plain borders to soften the edge of the centre panel. The cushion cover has a simple envelope closure at the back – also embroidered with feather stitch – and rag tassels at each corner.

SIZE:
30cm x 30cm (12in x12in)

THREADS
DMC stranded embroidery cotton: one skein each of turquoise blue 3766; green 3819

MATERIALS
➤ 50cm x 122cm (20in x 48in) of blue and white check furnishing cotton: approximate size of check 12mm (1/2in)
➤ Sewing thread to match the fabric
➤ Crewel needle, size 6
➤ Cushion pad, 33cm x 33cm (13in x 13in)

LAUNDRY BAG

A laundry bag is a practical asset for any bathroom or bedroom, especially in busy households. Made from check cotton, with a lively contrasting green lining, this version is roomy enough to hold lots of laundry and has a drawstring top; it can be hung behind the bedroom door as a pretty personal accessory. The bag is smocked across the top with honeycomb stitch, gathering the fabric into simple V-shaped patterns.

SIZE:
62cm (24^1/$_2$in) length,
54.5cm (21^1/$_2$in) width

THREADS
DMC stranded embroidery cotton:
one skein of green 913

MATERIALS
➤ 70cm (27in) of check Madras cotton, 114cm (45in) wide
➤ 60cm (24in) of contrast Madras cotton seersucker, 114cm (45in) wide, for the lining
➤ Crewel needle, size 6
➤ 2m (2^1/$_4$yd) contrast cord, 5mm (^{3}/$_{16}$in wide)
➤ Sewing thread to match the checked fabric

DAMASK SPOT CUSHION

Deeply textured honeycomb smocking combined with shiny glass beads produces a uniquely tactile, twinkling surface, as seen in the centre panel of this damask scatter cushion.

The panel is set in a plain border, softened at the edges with double feather stitch and iridescent pearl buttons in each corner. The cushion cover has a plain damask back, and is closed with a slip-stitched seam.

SIZE:
27cm x 25cm (10^{1}/$_{2}$in x 9^{3}/$_{4}$in)

THREADS
DMC stranded embroidery cotton: one skein of blue 747

MATERIALS
- Cream silk or polyester with damask spot 12mm (^{1}/$_{2}$in) diamond repeat: two pieces 29cm x 28cm (11^{1}/$_{2}$in x 11in) for the back and front; 46cm x 23cm (9in x 18in) for the centre panel
- Three pieces of calico, 29cm x 28cm (11^{1}/$_{2}$in x 11in) for the backing
- Silk sewing thread to match the silk fabric
- Blue glass beads; DMC 04828, one box
- Light silver glass beads; DMC 07317, one box
- Fine beading needle
- Crewel needle, size 7
- Four pearl buttons, 12mm (^{1}/$_{2}$in) diameter
- 30cm x 30cm (12in x 12in) cushion pad

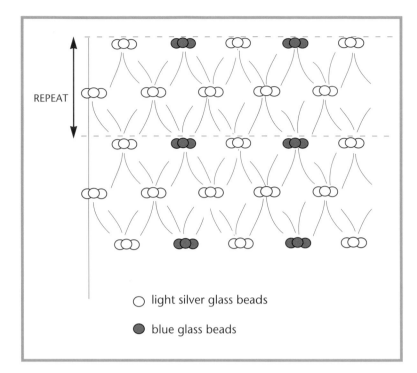

REPEAT

○ light silver glass beads

● blue glass beads

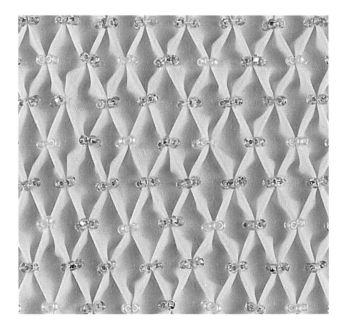

The smocking

1 Working on the centre panel and using silk sewing thread, begin working honeycomb smocking at the right-hand side, leaving margins of about 4cm (1½in) all round, depending on the size of the spot pattern. (See page 122 for how to work honeycomb stitch.) The finished smocking on this panel measures 14.5cm x 14cm (5¾in x 5½in).

Although it is quite simple to adjust different spot patterns, you may prefer to make the panel smaller or bigger to fit your particular fabric; one thing to bear in mind here is that honeycomb smocking seems to work best when the stitch is not too big and floppy.

Whatever you decide, begin at the top and work the first one or two rows of smocking, then measure across and adjust the width, if necessary, and check the length as well. If you need extra spots, you can always use some of the side margins, remembering to leave at least 2cm (¾in) seam allowances all round.

2 Following the bead pattern given in the diagram above left, complete the smocking, adding three beads (as shown in the pattern) to each honeycomb stitch.

3 Place the finished smocking right side down on a well-padded ironing board; pin to size and press very lightly.

On the right side, backstitch across the top and bottom folds 1cm (³⁄₈in) away from the smocking. Trim the fabric to 2.5cm (1in) all round.

Making the cushion cover panel

4 To complete the top section, place one of the pieces of calico and the silk front wrong sides together; tack, first diagonally across the shape, then around

the edges 1.5cm (⁵/₈in) in from the edge. In the centre of the calico, lightly draw a rectangle to the size of the smocked area. Then draw a second rectangle 1.5cm (⁵/₈in) inside. Tack around the larger rectangle 1.5cm (⁵/₈in) outside the pencil line. To cut away the centre fabric, use the diagonal tacked lines as a guide and snip carefully into the corners. Then, cut out the inner rectangle following the pencil lines (see right).

5 Fold the turnings to the wrong side and tack; on the right side, machine stitch close to the edge.

6 Place the border over the smocked panel; pin and tack all round. Using silk thread, hem the border to the panel, hiding the stitches just inside the folded edge. Neatly stitch the corners.

7 Tack the second piece of calico to the wrong side, to give support to the slightly stretchy smocked panel. Working through all layers, and using two strands of embroidery cotton in the needle, work double feather stitch (see page 127) around the smocking, stopping and starting the stitch at the corners. Finally, stitch the buttons to the corners using the blue embroidery thread. Remove all tacking stitches.

8 For the cushion cover back, place the remaining pieces of silk and calico wrong sides together, and tack as you did for the front.

Finishing the cushion

9 Place the front and back sections right sides together, tack, then machine stitch leaving an 18cm (7in) opening in one side. Fold under and tack the edges of the opening. Insert the cushion pad and slipstitch the opening closed. Remove the tacking stitches.

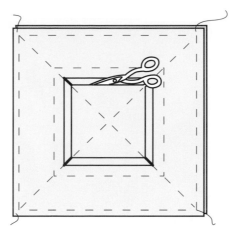

Cut away the centre fabric and snip the corners

TARTAN BOLSTER

Choose from the many colourful tartan silks on the market to create a bolster cover with your own smocking design. The finished effect of this type of smocking depends on the size and colour of the stripes which make up the tartan pattern, but once you've decided which parts to stitch, it's amazingly quick and easy to do. The transformation from plain, straightforward tartan to a pleated and stitched texture is quite astonishing.

  The finished bolster cover is made into a simple tube, slipped over a purchased foam base or bolster pad, and then tied stylishly at each end with large floppy bows made from the same tartan fabric.

SIZE:
66cm x 36cm (26in x 14in)

THREADS

DMC stranded embroidery cotton: one skein each of purple 333; green 943; yellow 783; cerise 917

MATERIALS

➤ Small bolster pad (or foam lumbar support) 33cm x 12cm (13in x 4³/4 in) diameter
➤ 84cm x 61cm (33in x 24in) of tartan dupion silk in mixed colours for the cover
➤ 76cm x 15cm (30in x 6in) of the same silk for the ties
➤ Sewing silk to match the fabric
➤ Crewel needle, size 7

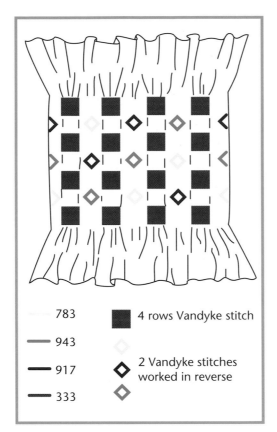

	783	■	4 rows Vandyke stitch
	943		
	917	◇	2 Vandyke stitches
	333		worked in reverse

Before you begin

When planning your own smocking designs on woven tartans or multiple check patterns for the first time, follow this simple principle. The idea is to smock small bands or blocks, repeated at regular intervals down the length of each tartan stripe and also across the stripes; in this way the width of the fabric is drawn up to measure the circumference of the bolster plus seam allowances at each side. See the diagram for the tartan bolster design given (left).

When you're choosing threads for smocking such richly-coloured fabrics, try much stronger colours than those in the tartan pattern – even vibrant shades – so that they will show up.

On the finished bolster, notice the smocked diamond shape and the interesting geometric effects that are created by the surrounding fabric folds.

The smocking

1 As silk frays very easily, it is always best to neaten the raw edges before you begin, either by machine zigzag or hand-stitched overcasting.

2 Following the diagram for the bolster design, the main blocks of smocking are worked in purple using Vandyke stitch and two strands of thread. The three individual diamonds, worked in each alternate row, are stitched in three different colours: red, yellow and green.

3 Decide which parts of your woven tartan you wish to smock and draw a rough plan as a reminder. On this fabric, the unworked tartan stripe measures 8cm (3¹/4in) across, and allows for six Vandyke stitches which measure 4.5cm (1¹/4in) across. The block therefore consists of four rows of six stitches, which are repeated four times over the same tartan intersection along the length of the

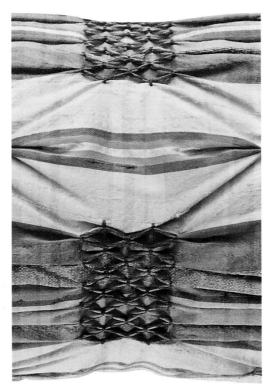

bolster. Adjust these dimensions to suit your own tartan fabric and the circumference of your bolster.

4 Working on the right side of the fabric, and beginning with a knot, work Vandyke stitch from right to left. At the end of the row, turn the embroidery upside down and work the next row back across the fabric and repeat as required. (See page 124 for how to work Vandyke stitch, and Vandyke stitch on tartan.)

5 Complete the smocking pattern. Check that the width matches the circumference of the bolster and, if needed, press on the wrong side; carefully stretch and pin the fabric to your ironing board and press it very lightly under a cloth.

Making the bolster

6 With right sides together and tartan stripes matching, pin and machine stitch the long edges, taking 1cm (³/₈in) seams. Press the seam open and turn to the right side. Complete the row of smocked diamonds over the seam.

7 At each end of the bolster cover, turn under the raw edges with 1cm (³/₈in) double seams. Pin and machine stitch. Slip the cover over the bolster, and at each end run a row of gathering stitches about 5cm (2in) from the smocking. Pull up the thread (see top right), even the gathers and knot firmly. This is the easiest way to ensure a neat finish for the ties.

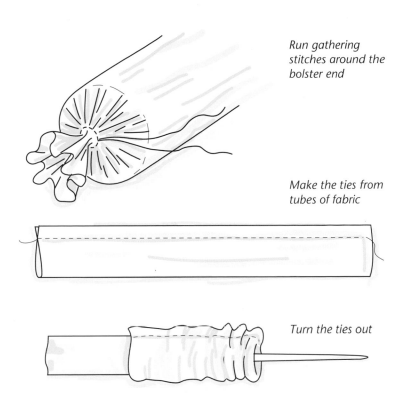

Run gathering stitches around the bolster end

Make the ties from tubes of fabric

Turn the ties out

Making the ties

8 Cut the fabric in half to give two pieces measuring 76cm x 7.5cm (30in x 3in). Pin each length of fabric right sides together and machine stitch the long edge, taking a 1cm (³/₈in) seam (see above). Finger press the seam open and place it in the centre of the tie. Stitch across one short end. Trim the corners and turn through to the right side, using a rouleau turner or the round end of a knitting needle to help you (see above). Press, turn in the raw edge of the opening and slipstitch to close. Complete the second tie in the same way. Wrap the ties over the gathering threads and finish with large floppy bows.

3 For children

BABY'S DRAWSTRING BAG

This roomy linen bag with its smocked drawstring top is designed to keep baby's toiletries close to hand, and would make an ideal gift for a mother-to-be or to welcome a new baby boy or girl.

The bag is made from a single piece of fabric – this includes the frill, which is neatened before the smocking is started. The edges of the bag are finished with deep pink ricrac braid – a strong contrast colour picked up from the smocked border, and repeated in the ribbon drawstrings.

Pearl buttons are another special feature. They are used to secure the side openings and to join the ends of the drawstring ribbons.

SIZE:
33cm deep x 40cm wide
(13in deep x 16in wide)

THREADS
DMC stranded embroidery cotton: one skein each of yellow 972; blues 341, 793; pink 602

MATERIALS
➤ 70cm x 42cm (28in x 16½in) of soft white linen
➤ 2m (2¼yd) deep pink ricrac braid
➤ One sheet smocking dots, 6mm x 1cm (¼in x ⅜in)
➤ 1.50m (1½yd) deep pink satin ribbon, 6mm (¼in) wide
➤ Four pearl buttons, 1cm (⅜in) diameter
➤ Four pearl buttons, 6cm (¼in) diameter
➤ Sewing thread to match the linen
➤ Crewel needle, size 5
➤ 40cm (16in) of white ribbon, 2cm (¾in) wide
➤ Ribbon threader

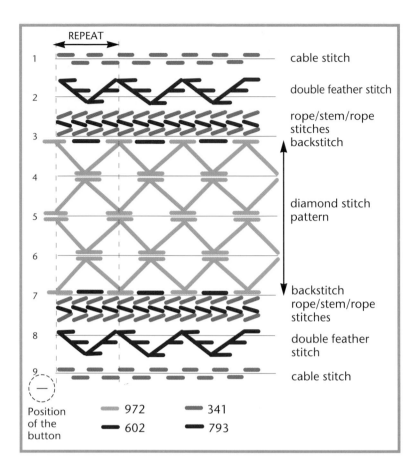

1	cable stitch
2	double feather stitch
3	rope/stem/rope stitches backstitch
4	
5	diamond stitch pattern
6	
7	backstitch rope/stem/rope stitches
8	double feather stitch
9	cable stitch

REPEAT

Position of the button

972   341
602   793

Preparing the fabric

1 Fold the linen in half, short edges together, and lightly press the fold to mark the centre of the fabric. Press a 3mm (1/8in) single turning to the wrong side on all four edges of the linen and tack.

On one short edge, pin and tack ricrac braid to the wrong side so that half the width of the braid shows on the right side and the other half covers the turning. Take the ricrac braid around the corners and along both long edges for 14cm (5¹/2in). In the same way, attach the remaining braid to the other short edge, taking it along both long edges to just beyond the centre line (see below left). Working from the right side, machine stitch close to the edge. Remove the tacking stitches.

The smocking

2 Apply 9 rows of smocking dots to the wrong side of both short edges of the prepared linen, placing the top row 4.5cm (1³/4in) from the top edge and leaving a 1cm (³/8in) fabric allowance at each side. Gather the dots in the usual way, and pull them up to measure 12.5cm (5in) at the top edge and 18cm (7in) across the bottom. Even out the gathers so that they fan out neatly.

3 Using three strands of thread for the smocking, begin by working chevron stitch in the diamond pattern, as shown on the smocking chart given above left. (For how to work the smocking stitches, see page 118 onwards.) Now work the double bands of stem stitch at the top and bottom of the diamond pattern, and then the rope stitch between. To soften the edges of the diamond band, work backstitch over the gathers in between the stitches.

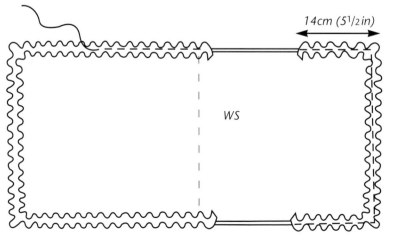

14cm (5¹/2in)

WS

Attach the braid as shown

Now work the top and bottom bands of cable stitch, adjusting the tension as required to give the correct shape.

Finish the smocking with the two rows of double feather stitch, again adjusting the tension to fit.

4 Complete the smocking on the second side, and remove the gathering threads. Lightly steam press the smocking on the wrong side, pinning it out to measure 15cm (6in) across the top 20cm (8in) across the bottom.

A useful tip for pressing bands of smocking is to pin it to your ironing board with the lower edge of the smocking level with the inner edge of the ironing board. This will allow you to press the smocking without creasing the gathered fabric below.

Applying the drawstring channel

5 Cut two 16cm (6¹⁄₄in) lengths of the white ribbon. Fold in the two short edges on each piece and pin to the wrong side behind the top band of smocking. Backstitch in place along the long edges only, taking the stitches through the top layer of the gathers so that the stitching does not show on the right side.

Making the bag

6 With right sides outside, fold the linen along the centre crease line, then pin and tack the two side edges together, sandwiching the ricrac braid between so that it makes the same pretty edging as around the top opening.

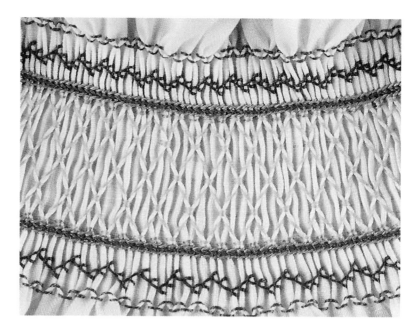

Machine stitch, leaving a 14cm (5¹⁄₂in) opening at the top of the bag.

Just below the band of smocking, stitch the larger pearl buttons to the bag, one behind the other, to secure the bottom of each side opening. To make the drawstring, cut the pink ribbon in half and thread each length through the channel in opposite directions (see page 137). Secure the ends by placing them together and stitching on the smaller buttons, one behind the other, about 3cm (1¹⁄₄in) from the end. Cut the raw edges of the ribbon at an angle to finish (see below).

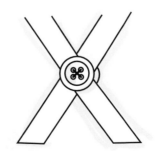

Secure the ends of the ribbon with two buttons

BABY'S BONNET

This is a 'wrap-around' bonnet style – overlapped and buttoned at the back for easy adjustment. It has a softly gathered frill, to protect young eyes from the sun, and is fully lined. The main bonnet is smocked in colours picked up from the lawn print, and ties under the chin with a pretty bow. Its prettiness is slightly reminiscent of the Kate Greenaway style of bonnet, and those worn by American frontiers-people.

The bonnet could be made for a christening or other special event, in plain lawn perhaps – and when the baby's outgrown it, it can be kept as a treasured keepsake that's been made with love.

SIZE:	**MATERIALS**
to fit a baby age six months	➤ 50cm (20in) of floral lawn 137cm (54in) wide
	➤ Two 1cm (³/₈in) buttons
THREADS	➤ Crewel needle, size 8
DMC stranded embroidery cotton: one skein each of greens 3810, 964; yellow 445; pink 602	➤ One sheet smocking dots: 6mm x 1cm (¹/₄in x ³/₈in)
	➤ Tracing paper
	➤ Sewing thread to match lawn

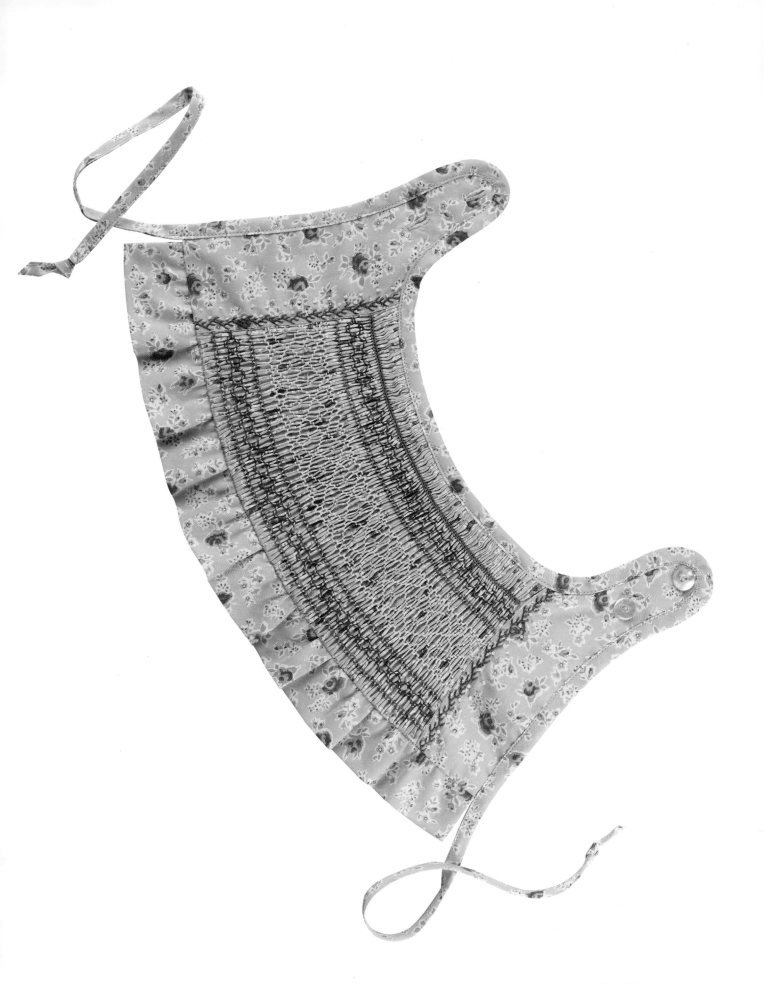

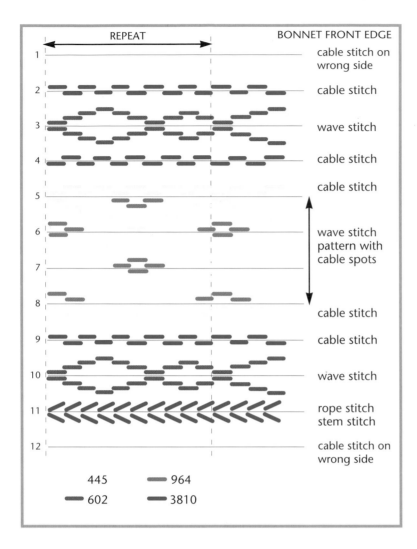

Row	Stitch
1	cable stitch on wrong side
2	cable stitch
3	wave stitch
4	cable stitch
5	cable stitch
6	wave stitch pattern with cable spots
7	
8	cable stitch
9	cable stitch
10	wave stitch
11	rope stitch stem stitch
12	cable stitch on wrong side

REPEAT — BONNET FRONT EDGE

445   964
602   3810

The pattern

1 Trace the bonnet pattern given opposite once for the lining. Trace the pattern a second time, extending it at the centre line by 24cm (9½in), to allow for the smocking gathers: cut out. Add the grain lines and balance marks to both paper patterns and then cut out the pieces from the lawn. Keep the remaining lawn, which will be needed later for the frill and combined binding and ties.

The smocking

2 From the sheet of smocking dots, cut out twelve rows, 74cm x 12cm (29½in x 4¾in). Pin them to the wrong side of the main bonnet section, between the marks shown on the pattern. Transfer the dots using a medium dry iron. Using a long length of sewing cotton to span each row and with a large knot at one end, gather the fabric by picking up a small amount of fabric under each dot. Pull up the gathers tightly at first and then release them so that they measure 24cm (9½in). Knot the threads firmly in pairs, and even out the gathers.

3 Following the smocking chart above left and working from the right side, begin by smocking the centre band using two strands of yellow 445 for the wave stitch pattern and three strands of green 964 for the cable spots between. (See page 118 onwards for how to work the stitches.)

4 Working towards the front edge of the bonnet, smock the upper border using two strands of green 3810 for the cable stitch and pink 602 for the diamond pattern, keeping an even tension.

Working towards the neck edge of the bonnet, and using two strands of thread (for this and also for the remaining embroidery), complete the lower border but with a slightly tighter tension.

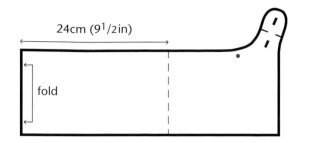

24cm (9$\frac{1}{2}$in)

fold

Baby's bonnet pattern

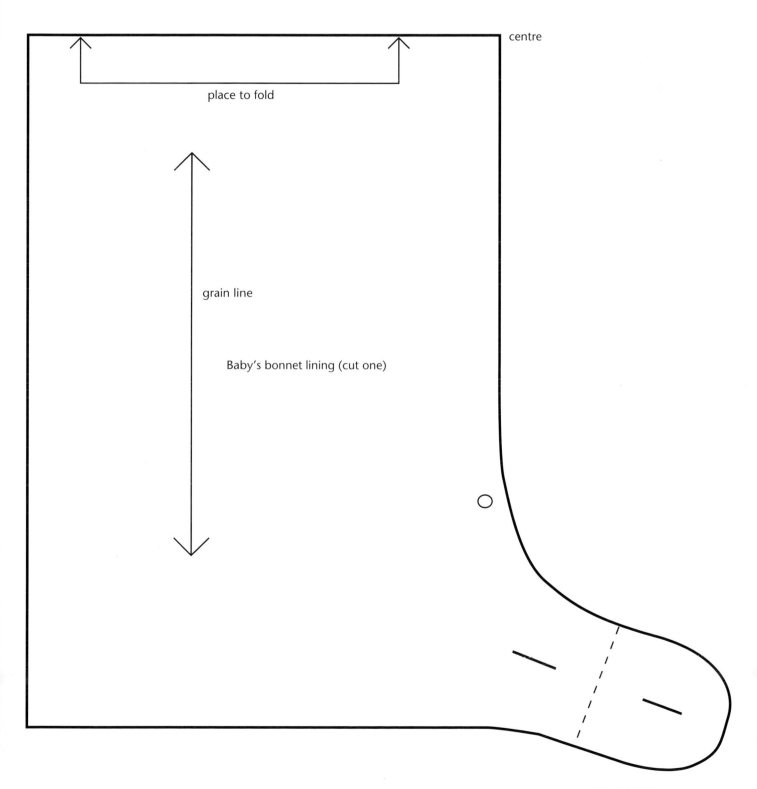

centre

place to fold

grain line

Baby's bonnet lining (cut one)

Finally, work the top rows of stem and rope stitch with a firm tension. Controlling the tension in this way helps to shape the bonnet into the neck.

5 On the wrong side of the smocking, work rows 1 and 12 with cable stitch. This helps to hold the gathers evenly when you come to make up the bonnet. Remove the gathering threads.

Decorating the side edges

6 At each side of the smocking, make a tiny tuck in the fabric towards the centre, placing the folded edge level with the smocking, and machine stitch across on the right side. Working close to the edge, embroider a row of double feather stitch in pink and, below this, work two rows of french knots in yellow. Repeat on the opposite side.

The frill

7 From doubled fabric, cut out a bias strip measuring 46cm x 4.5cm (18in x 1³/₄in), placing one long edge to the fold. With right sides together, pin and stitch the short edges. Trim across the corners and turn right side out; press. With raw edges even, run a row of gathering stitches just inside the seam allowance.

8 With right sides together, pin the frill to the bonnet front edge, placing it 6mm (¹/₄in) inside the outer edge of the bonnet (see above left). Pull up the gathering thread to fit, even out the gathers and tack across. Place the bonnet lining on top, right sides together, pin and machine stitch through all layers.

9 Fold the lining away from the frill and, working from the right side of the lining, machine stitch through the existing seam (see left). Refold with the frill and lining in the correct position; press.

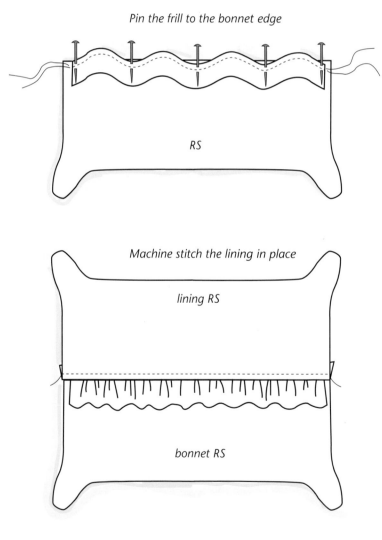

Pin the frill to the bonnet edge

RS

Machine stitch the lining in place

lining RS

bonnet RS

10 Run a gathering thread along the neck edge of the lining, between the points marked on the pattern and 2cm (³/4in) below the raw edge. Pull up the gathers evenly so that the lining fits the bonnet, and knot the thread firmly. With the raw edges matching, tack around the sides and back of the bonnet.

Ties and binding

11 Cut two bias strips 69cm x 3cm (27in x 1¹/4in), and join the two pieces together to make a long length. With right sides together, pin and machine stitch on the straight grain (see page 136). Press the seam open and trim.

12 With the wrong sides together, pin and machine stitch the bias binding to the bonnet, beginning at the centre back. Take the binding around the back, button tabs and along the neck edges, leaving 28cm (11in) ties extending at each side. Fold the binding to the right side, then pin, tack and machine stitch along the ties and binding in a continuous line, stitching close to the edge. Finally, knot the raw ends of each tie. Remove the tacking stitches, and press if needed.

Buttons and buttonholes

13 Place the paper pattern on the right side of the bonnet tab and transfer the position of the buttonholes by marking the length of each one with pins (inserted through the pattern); then lightly draw in the horizontal line with a soft pencil.

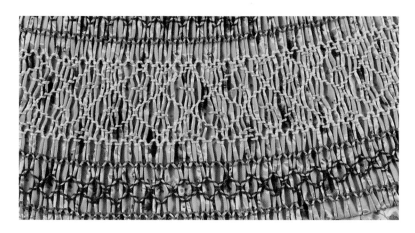

14 To prepare the buttonhole for hand stitching, begin by working running stitches around the line to form a neat rectangle, using matching sewing thread. Cut through both layers of fabric along the line using small embroidery scissors, being careful not to cut into the stitches. Slip the button through the slit to check for size.

15 Work close buttonhole stitch around the opening taking the needle over the running stitches, back through the centre opening and through the looped thread. Pull the thread fairly firmly, keeping the pearl edge of the stitch neatly on the inside edge of the buttonhole (see page 134). At each end of the buttonhole work one or two straight stitches for extra strength. Finish off on the wrong side and trim any loose threads.

16 To mark the position for the buttons, simply overlap the tabs with the buttonholed tab on top, and pin through the centre of each buttonhole. Attach the buttons to finish.

BABY'S DRESS

It is always fun to receive clothes for a new baby, but a dress that has been specially made is particularly welcome. This little dress, both pretty and practical, is made with a dark background fabric; I chose this specially to show up the smocking, which is worked mainly in bright yellow with highlights in red. Of course, it can also be made in any other colour combination, but it does show how striking areas of mainly single-coloured smocking can be.

The dress is one of the easiest styles to make – its plain neck and armholes are simply bound around the edges, the straight-cut skirt is gathered at the waist and there is a centre-back buttoned opening. The length can be adjusted to fit the baby, and given a deeper hem if preferred.

SIZE:
to fit a baby age six months; 61cm (24in) chest, 41cm (16in) length

THREADS
DMC coton à broder: one skein each of yellow 444 and red 666

MATERIALS
➤ 60cm (24in) of fine cotton, 137cm (54in) wide
➤ Two 1cm (3/8in) buttons
➤ Crewel needle, size 6
➤ One sheet smocking dots (pale blue or yellow for darker fabrics): 6mm x 1cm (1/4in x 3/8in)
➤ Tracing paper
➤ Toning bias binding, 12cm (1/2in) wide
➤ Sewing threads to match fabric

The bodice pattern

1 Trace the bodice pattern given opposite, following the outline for the back. Transfer the grainlines, balance marks and annotation, and cut out. On a larger piece of paper, trace the bodice front outline and extend it by 12.5cm (5in) at the centre front, to allow fullness for the smocking gathers. Transfer the marks and cut out.

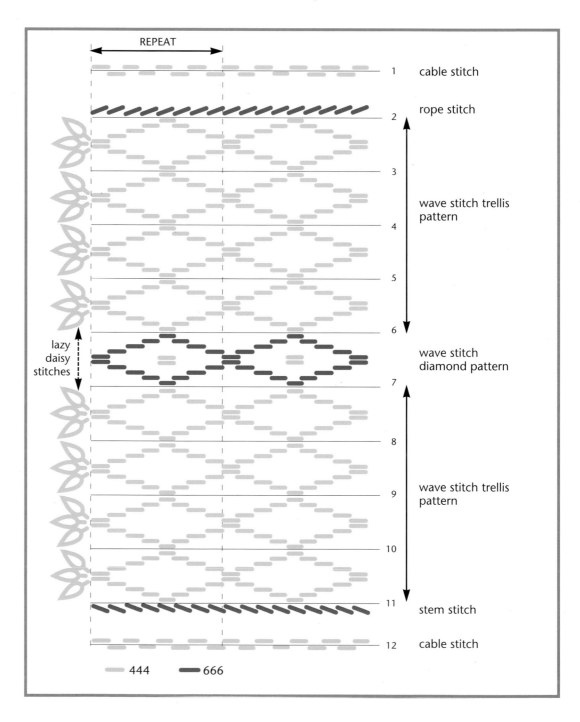

REPEAT

1   cable stitch

2   rope stitch

3

wave stitch trellis pattern

4

5

6

wave stitch diamond pattern

7

lazy daisy stitches

8

wave stitch trellis pattern

9

10

11   stem stitch

12   cable stitch

444   666

2 From the dress fabric, cut out the bodice back section and the extended bodice front section as instructed. For the front bodice lining, fold back the extended pattern and cut out in the same fabric, placing the centre front to a fold. Cut along the back centre fold for the opening.

The smocking

3 From the sheet of smocking dots, cut out 12 rows: 74cm x 12cm (29$\frac{1}{4}$in x 4$\frac{3}{4}$in). Place the dots centrally on the wrong side of the bodice front, pin to hold and press with a medium dry iron.

4 Use long lengths of sewing thread, measured across the smocking panel plus extra for handling. Begin each thread with a large knot and run gathering stitches along each row. Pick up a small amount of fabric beneath the dots, and leave the thread loose at the end of the row.

Pull up the gathers tightly, to set the folds, and then release them to measure 9cm (3$\frac{1}{2}$in). Knot the threads firmly in pairs, and even out the gathers.

12.5cm (5in)

fold

Baby's dress bodice pattern

back neck

front neck edge

Baby's dress bodice front (cut one), bodice back (cut one)

back armhole

front armhole

grain line

smocking dots

centre back and front place to fold

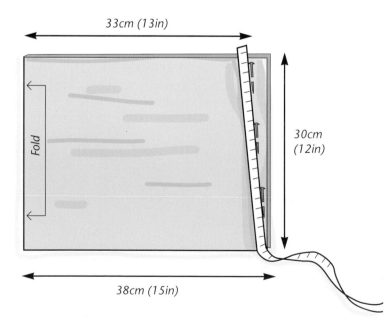

5 Following the smocking chart given on page 70 and the stitch diagrams on page 118 onwards, begin by working the top and bottom rows of cable stitch in yellow. Then smock the two bands of wave stitch trellis pattern in yellow, as shown, followed by the centre band of wave stitch diamond pattern in red. To complete the centre band, work two horizontal straight stitches (above each other) over the two centre folds of each diamond, beginning and finishing each pair separately.

6 Using red thread, finish the smocking by working above row 2 in rope stitch and below row 11 in stem stitch, keeping an even tension. On the wrong side, work cable stitch at the neck and waist edges, to hold the folds neatly in the seam allowance. Remove the gathering threads. Using yellow thread, work groups of lazy daisy stitch at each side of the panel, as shown in the smocking chart.

Bodice front lining

7 With wrong sides together, pin the bodice lining to the bodice front and tack around the edges. When making up the dress, treat the two layers as one.

Dress skirt

8 The skirt can easily be cut out without a paper pattern, using a tape measure and pins.

Fold the remaining fabric on the straight grain to give two rectangles measuring 30cm x 38cm (12in x 15in) across for the skirt front and back. Mark the corners with pins and cut out the two pieces. Mark the top edge of each rectangle 33cm (13in) from the fold and then, using your tape measure and pins, mark the diagonal line for the skirt outside edges and cut to shape (see left).

Shape the fabric for the skirt

33cm (13in)

Fold

30cm (12in)

38cm (15in)

9 Machine a line of gathering stitches across the front waist edge, just inside the seam allowance. Pull up the gathers so that the skirt waist fits the front bodice waist, 34cm (13^1/$_2$in). Ease the gathers towards the centre, away from the side seams.

10 With right sides together and waist edges even, pin and tack the bodice to the skirt. Machine stitch, then press the seam towards the bodice.

11 On the skirt back, cut a 10cm (4in) centre opening at the waist edge. Gather both sides of the skirt to fit the bodice back sections at the waist. Pin, tack and machine stitch; press the seam towards the bodice.

The back opening

12 To neaten the back opening, cut a strip of fabric for the facing measuring 46cm x 4.5cm (18in x 1^3/$_4$in). Place the right side of the facing to the wrong side of the dress and pin. Machine stitch, pivoting the fabric around the needle at the lower point of the opening before stitching the second side. Press the seam outwards. Make a narrow single turning on the facing and fold it over to the right side. Pin and machine stitch.

To make the overlap, fold under the facing on the right side of the bodice and then press the fold at the lower point of the opening. Trim the neck edge if needed.

Shoulder seams

13 Place the back and front bodice sections right sides together. Pin and machine stitch the shoulders, taking 1cm (3$/$8in) seams. Press the seams open and neaten the edges with zigzag stitch (see page 132).

Side seams

14 Place the dress front and back right sides together; pin and stitch the side seams from the underarm to the hem in one continuous movement. Press the seams open and neaten them as before.

Neck and armholes

15 Bind the neck edge and the armholes with bias binding (see page 136). At the neck edge, pin the binding in place, right sides together, extending it by 1cm (3$/$8in) at each side of the back opening. Machine stitch, taking 6mm (1$/$4in) seams. At the opening, turn in the extended binding and then fold the binding to the wrong side; pin in place and slipstitch by hand.

16 To bind the armholes, begin by turning under the raw edge of the binding, pin it in place and overlap to finish. Fold over the binding to the wrong side and slipstitch as before.

Buttons and buttonholes

17 Two buttons are used to close the opening. Mark the horizontal position of the two buttonholes on the overlap: one at the neck and one at the waist, 6mm (1$/$4in) in from the edge. Make the buttonholes and sew on the buttons as for the baby's bonnet on page 67.

The hem

18 First make a 6mm (1$/$4in) turning to the wrong side and press. Then turn up 3cm (1^1/$_4$in), pin and slipstitch in place, easing the slight fullness at the side seams. Remove the tacking stitches and press to finish.

GIRL'S BAG

My inspiration for the girl's bag, and this particular style of smocking, came from seeing a photograph of an African bag; it was similarly shaped and woven, I suspect, from multicoloured grasses. The main impression was of vertical lines superimposed with horizontal bands of zigzag patterns. Vertical lines were easily interpreted with the fabric folds, and the bands across were filled with geometric line patterns worked in 'stretched-out' wave stitch, using just two colours. This stitch gives an attractive two-colour effect, and is really easy and very quick to work, so that reasonably large areas can be smocked this way. A series of scatter cushions for a sofa, perhaps?

The bag is fully lined, and bound around the top edge in a contrast colour. Its short shoulder strap, made from twisted embroidery threads, and the bottom tassel, are decorated with large beads, echoing the ethnic quality I so admired in the African bag.

SIZE:
Length 31cm (12in); across the top 28cm (11in); across the bottom 13cm (5in)

THREADS
DMC stranded embroidery cotton: two skeins each of dark green 3808, red 350

MATERIALS
➤ 76cm x 36cm (30in x 14in) of medium weight pale khaki cotton for the bag front
➤ 33cm x 33cm (13in x 13in) of pale khaki cotton for the bag back
➤ Two contrast pieces of lightweight cotton (red and yellow) each 33cm x 33cm (13in x 13in) for the lining
➤ Contrast (red) bias binding, 2.5cm (1in) wide
➤ Crewel needle, size 5
➤ Large crewel (or chenille) needle
➤ Large bodkin
➤ Sewing threads to match the fabrics
➤ Two sheets of smocking dots, 8mm x 12mm (5/16in x 1/2in)
➤ Three large beads, 2cm (3/4in) diameter, for decoration
➤ Fabric marking pen

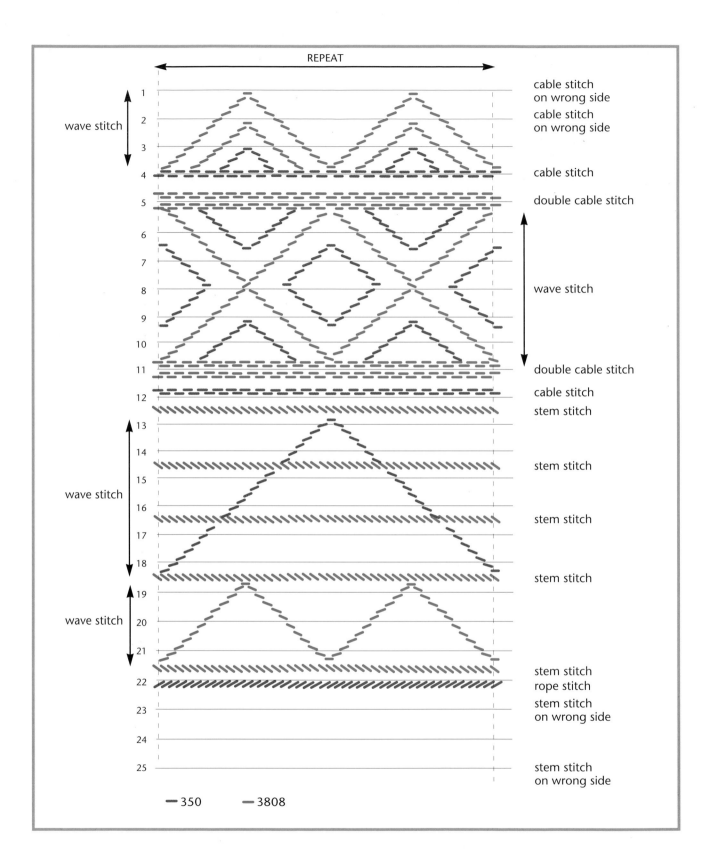

REPEAT

1	cable stitch on wrong side
2	cable stitch on wrong side
3	
4	cable stitch
5	double cable stitch
6	
7	
8	wave stitch
9	
10	
11	double cable stitch
12	cable stitch
	stem stitch
13	
14	
15	stem stitch
16	stem stitch
17	
18	stem stitch
19	
20	
21	
22	stem stitch / rope stitch
23	stem stitch on wrong side
24	
25	stem stitch on wrong side

wave stitch

wave stitch

wave stitch

— 350   — 3808

The smocking

1 From the two sheets of smocking dots, cut out 25 rows to fit the fabric dimensions. You will have to cut the paper and evenly butt the edges together; secure them either with small pieces of sticky tape on the wrong side, or with pins on the right side – removing the pins as you press, of course. Place the paper on the wrong side of the fabric, 3cm (1¼in) below the top edge and 2cm (⅝in) inside the bottom edge, leaving 2cm (⅝in) seam allowances at each side. Pin through the edges and transfer the dots using a warm dry iron.

2 Gather the dots using lengths of thread the width of the fabric, then pull the threads up in pairs, gathering the fabric tightly. Release the gathers to measure 24cm (9½in) across the top and 13cm (5in) across the bottom, and knot the threads firmly.

3 Following the smocking chart given opposite, and working with two strands of thread throughout, work the design downwards from the top to the centre row of red cable stitch, smocking with an even tension. (See page 118 onwards for the stitch diagrams.)

4 Next, work the horizontal rows of stem stitch; as you work towards the bottom of the bag, gradually increase the tension to shape the sides. Work the zigzag patterns in wave stitch to complete the smocking.
   On the wrong side of the fabric and using matching sewing thread, work cable stitch just above rows 1 and 2, and very tight stem stitch close to rows 23 and 25, to help shape the pointed base.

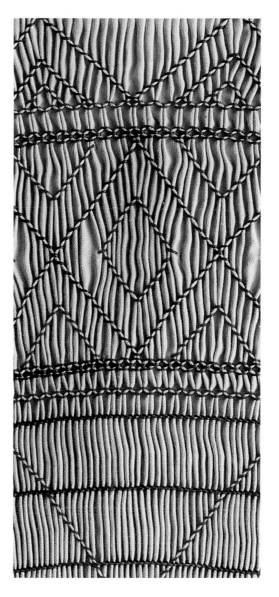

reverse from centre

row 20

Trace line for pointed end of bag

Making the bag

5 Remove the gathering threads. Pin the smocking to your ironing board, right side down, stretching the top edge to measure 30.5cm (12in) and the bottom to 11.5cm (4½in), inside the seam allowances. Lightly steam press.

6 Pin the bag front on the back fabric, right sides together, and cut out to shape. Using the back section as a template, cut out two pieces for the lining.

7 To shape the bottom of the bag, trace the pointed outline given above left, add the balance marks and cut out. With the bag sections pinned right sides together (smocked side facing upwards), place the pointed template on top, matching the balance marks to row 20. Lightly trace around with the marking pen to give the pointed seamline.

8 Machine stitch around the bag, taking a 12mm (½in) seam and leaving the top open. Trim the seam to 8mm (5/16in) and turn through to the right side. Trim the top edge to 8mm (5/16in).

9 Make the lining in the same way as the bag, shaping the pointed end and trimming the seam, but do not turn through. Place the lining inside the bag, smoothing it to shape and fitting it into the pointed end. Trim the top edge level with the bag. Pin the lining to the main fabric and tack around the top edge, then cover with contrast bias binding (see page 136).

The tassel

10 Decorate the pointed end of the bag with a large bead knotted onto a length of plaited thread. Cut nine 23cm (9in) lengths of the green embroidery cotton.

Using a large crewel (or chenille) needle, pass each length through the centre bottom seam, threading them through the same hole. Plait the threads together (see right) and pass them through a large bead. Knot 2.5cm (1in) from the end, then trim and fray the loose threads.

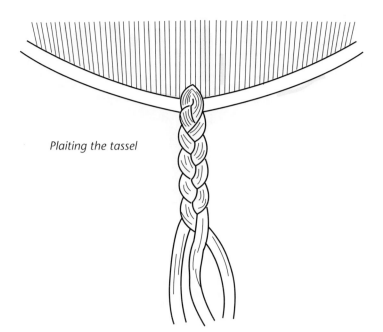

Plaiting the tassel

The bag strap

11 This is made by twisting together lengths of embroidery cotton to produce a firm cord. The joy of this type of cord is that it can be made to match exactly the colour of the smocking.

For a two-tone twisted cord, cut three 2m (78in) lengths of green and red embroidery cotton. Fold each group in half and knot the colours together, placing the knots in the centre and the loops at the ends.

With a pencil in each loop (see below) – either get someone to hold one pencil, or trap it in something like a drawer – twist the threads together until the cord twists tightly on itself. Keeping the cord taut, bring the pencils together and shake it quickly and vigorously, like cracking a whip. Remove the pencils, and wrap the ends of the cord with small pieces of sticky tape to stop them unravelling.

Using a large bodkin, make a hole in each side seam, level with the green cable stitching. Thread the ends of the cord through each hole, and finish on the outside with a large bead, as for the tassel.

Making a two-tone cord

NINE-PATCH PILLOW

Nine patches of bright, contrasting fabrics, colourfully smocked and embroidered and then pieced into a checked background, make a rich mixture for this patchwork pillow.

Some of the designs are taken from other projects in the book but are worked here in different colours. Using embroidery as a natural complement to smocking is a throwback to traditional times when country folk embroidered motifs on their smocks, usually to illustrate their trade.

The pillow opens on both side edges, and each edge is fastened with two fabric ties in contrasting colours. As an alternative to nine patches, you may prefer to make a standard cushion cover using only four.

SIZE:
46cm x 46cm (18in x 18in)

THREADS
DMC stranded embroidery cotton: one skein each of yellows 307, 741, 972, 3802; pink 3607; purples 333, 340, 552; greens 227, 910, 924, 959, 3765, 3809; reds 601, 718

MATERIALS
- Fabrics for smocked patches: 31cm x 13cm (12in x 5in), one piece each in yellow, green, red and blue
- Fabrics for embroidered patches: 13cm x 13cm (5in x 5in), two pieces in red, one each in yellow, blue and green
- 50cm x 112cm (20in x 44in) of checked (green/purple) Madras cotton
- 50cm x 50cm (20in x 20in) of heavyweight synthetic wadding
- 50cm x 50cm (20in x 20in) of unbleached calico
- Contrast fabrics: four pieces 48cm x 6.5cm (19in x 2 1/2 in) for the opening facings; 16 pieces 15cm x 6.5cm (6in x 2 1/2 in) for the ties
- One sheet of smocking dots, 6mm x 1cm (1/4 in x 3/8 in)
- Sewing thread to match the fabrics
- Crewel needle, size 7
- Cushion pad, 41cm (16in) square

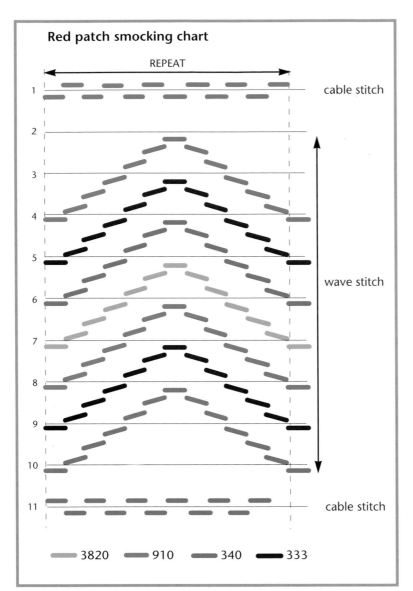

Red patch smocking chart

REPEAT

1   cable stitch

wave stitch

cable stitch

3820   910   340   333

The smocking

1 Following the instructions given for the perfumed drawer sachets on page 98, apply 11 rows of smocking dots to the red and green patches. Notice that these two smocking patterns are worked in different colours for the pillow. For the smocking, follow the colour guides given left and opposite. Smocking charts for the yellow and blue patches are given on pages 84 and 85. These are adaptations from the girl's bag and the baby's drawstring bag on pages 74 and 58; complete the smocking as instructed in the relevant projects.

2 Remove the gathering threads and lightly steam press on the wrong side so that the smocking measures 10cm x 10cm (4in x 4in).

The embroidery

3 Begin by marking with pins a 10cm (4in) square in the centre of each piece of fabric, then tack the outline as a guide for the embroidery.

4 Trace the full-size (black-line) motifs given on pages 86–89, and transfer them to the right side of the fabric using carbon paper (see page 137). Using three strands of thread throughout, work the embroidery following the annotated stitch and colour guides. Lightly steam press the finished motifs on the wrong side.

Making the pillow

5 From the check cotton, cut out the pillow back following the straight grain: 48cm x 48cm (19in x 19in). For the pillow front, cut out four strips (A, B, C and D) 41cm x 6.5cm (16in x 2$\frac{1}{2}$in); two strips (E and F) 48cm x 6.5cm (19cm x 2$\frac{1}{2}$in); six strips (G) 13cm x 6.5cm (5in x 2$\frac{1}{2}$in). Seam allowances of 12cm ($\frac{1}{2}$in) are included in these measurements.

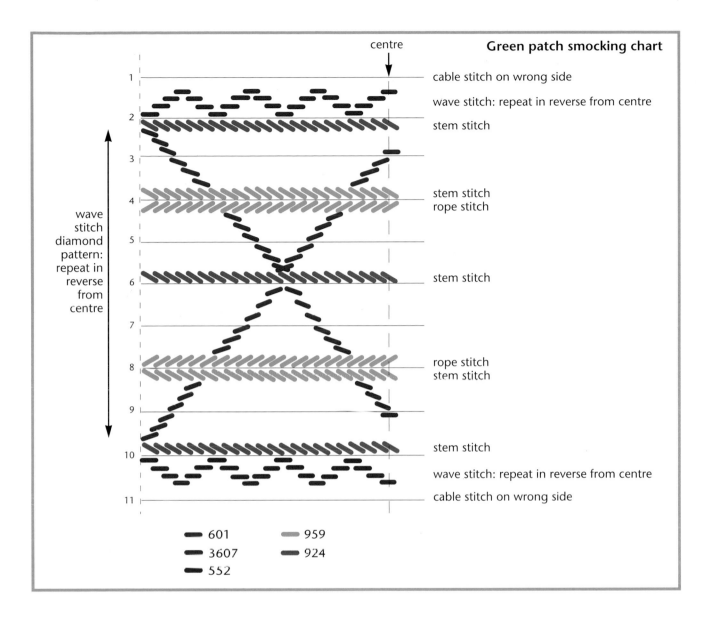

centre

Green patch smocking chart

1 — cable stitch on wrong side

wave stitch: repeat in reverse from centre

2 — stem stitch

3

4 — stem stitch
rope stitch

wave
stitch
diamond
pattern:
repeat in
reverse
from
centre

5

6 — stem stitch

7

8 — rope stitch
stem stitch

9

10 — stem stitch

wave stitch: repeat in reverse from centre

11 — cable stitch on wrong side

— 601   — 959
— 3607   — 924
— 552

6 Following the positioning guide (see right), first lay out all the pieces in sequence. Begin piecing them together, starting with the top row of patches. Pin, tack and machine stitch the side edges together in this sequence: 1, G, 2, G, 3. Join the remaining two rows in the same way. Trim and press the seams open. When you are stitching, use the checks as a guide for the seamlines.

7 Next, join strips A and B in the same way, then strips C and D. Finally, join the side pieces E and F to complete piecing the nine-patch pillow front.

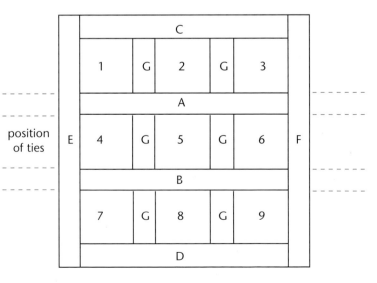

position of ties

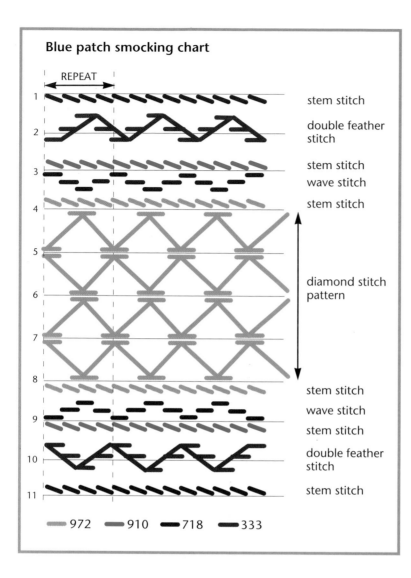

Blue patch smocking chart

REPEAT

1 — stem stitch
2 — double feather stitch
3 — stem stitch / wave stitch
4 — stem stitch
5
6 — diamond stitch pattern
7
8 — stem stitch / wave stitch / stem stitch
9
10 — double feather stitch
11 — stem stitch

— 972 — 910 — 718 — 333

Adding the quilting ties

8 Place the calico on a flat surface with the wadding on top, smoothing it from the centre outwards. Position the patchwork on top; pin and tack across the centre in both directions and then around the edges.

Using two six-strands of mixed coloured threads in the needle, work quilting ties in the corners of each patch as shown (see below right), cutting them back to about 2cm (³/4in) long. Trim the edges of the calico and wadding to the same size as the checked fabric. Leave the tacking stitches in at this stage.

Finishing the pillow

9 With the pillow front and back right sides together, pin and stitch the top and bottom edges. Turn through to the right side, and press the seamed edges. Place pairs of the opening facing right sides together, join the two short edges to form a circle and press the seams open. With right sides together, pin and stitch the facing to the opening edges. Fold to the wrong side, and press the seam.

10 Make the ties by placing pairs of fabric right sides together, and stitching around three sides. Trim across the corners, turn through the open short side and press.

11 Make a single turning on each facing and pin to the wrong side of the opening. Insert the ties under the facing, aligning them with the spaces between the patches, and tack to secure. Refold the ties so that they are pointing upwards, and tack. On the right side, machine stitch close to the patches, securing the facing and ties at the same time.

Remove all tacking stitches. Insert the cushion and knot the ties to finish.

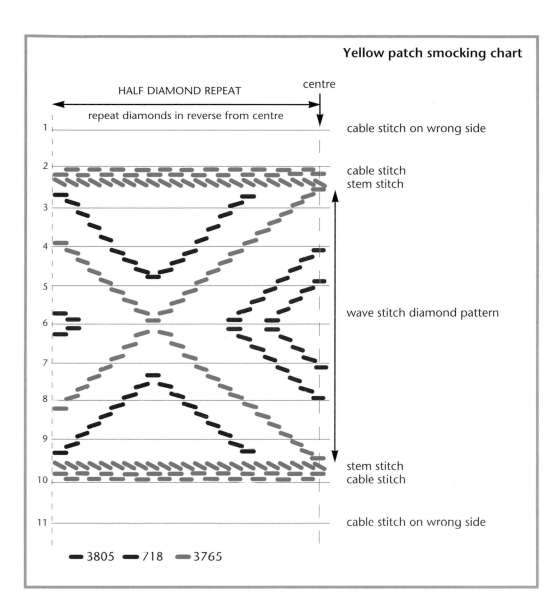

Yellow patch smocking chart

HALF DIAMOND REPEAT

repeat diamonds in reverse from centre

centre

1 — cable stitch on wrong side

2 — cable stitch
stem stitch

3

4

5 — wave stitch diamond pattern

6

7

8

9

10 — stem stitch
cable stitch

11 — cable stitch on wrong side

━ 3805 ━ 718 ━ 3765

Knotting the quilting ties

Red patch trace pattern

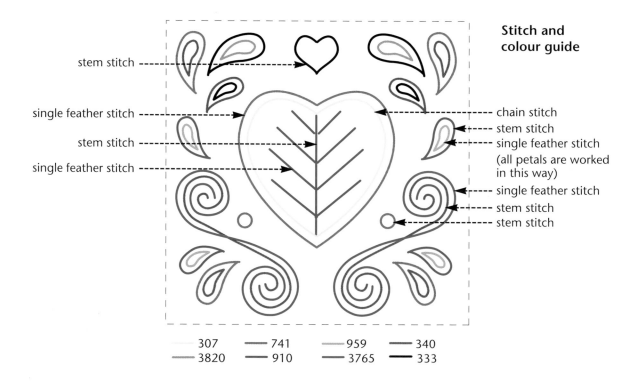

Stitch and colour guide

stem stitch

single feather stitch

stem stitch

single feather stitch

chain stitch

stem stitch

single feather stitch
(all petals are worked
in this way)

single feather stitch

stem stitch

stem stitch

307 — 741 — 959 — 340
— 3820 — 910 — 3765 — 333

Yellow patch trace pattern

Stitch and colour guide

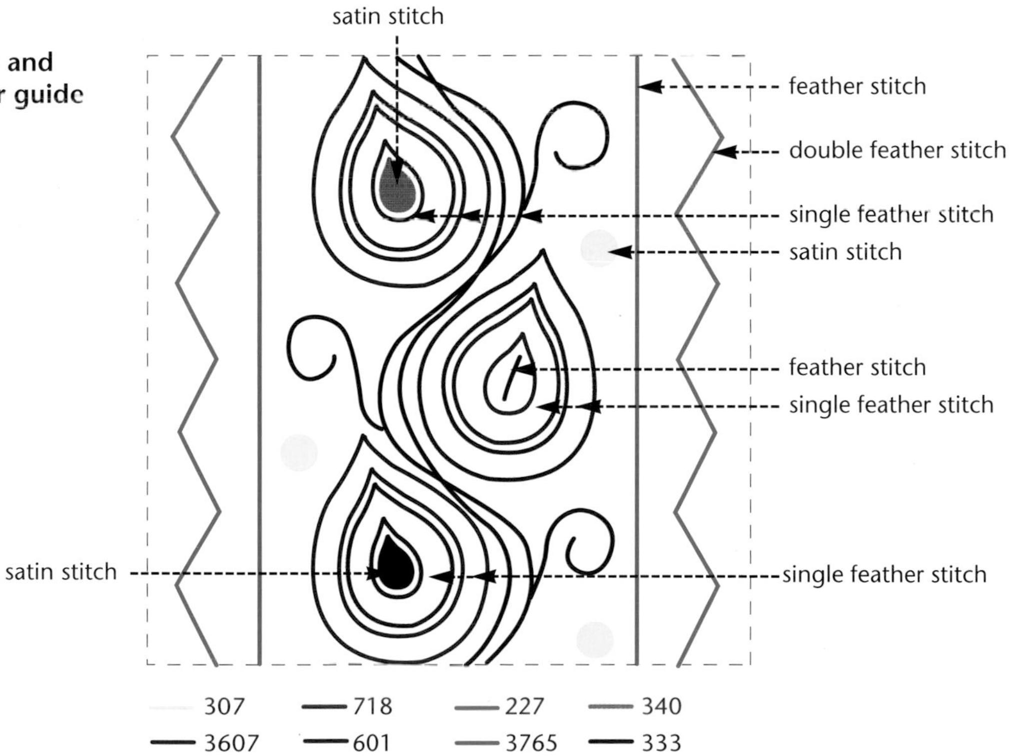

satin stitch

feather stitch

double feather stitch

single feather stitch

satin stitch

feather stitch

single feather stitch

satin stitch

single feather stitch

	307		718		227		340
	3607		601		3765		333

Stitch and colour guide

Red patch trace pattern

single feather stitch   feather stitch

— 3820   — 340   — 333

Blue patch trace pattern
Work in single feather stitch except for the areas marked

Stitch and colour guide

feather stitch   all green leaves in feather stitch

307   — 741   — 552   — 227   — 3809
— 972   — 601   — 3805   — 910

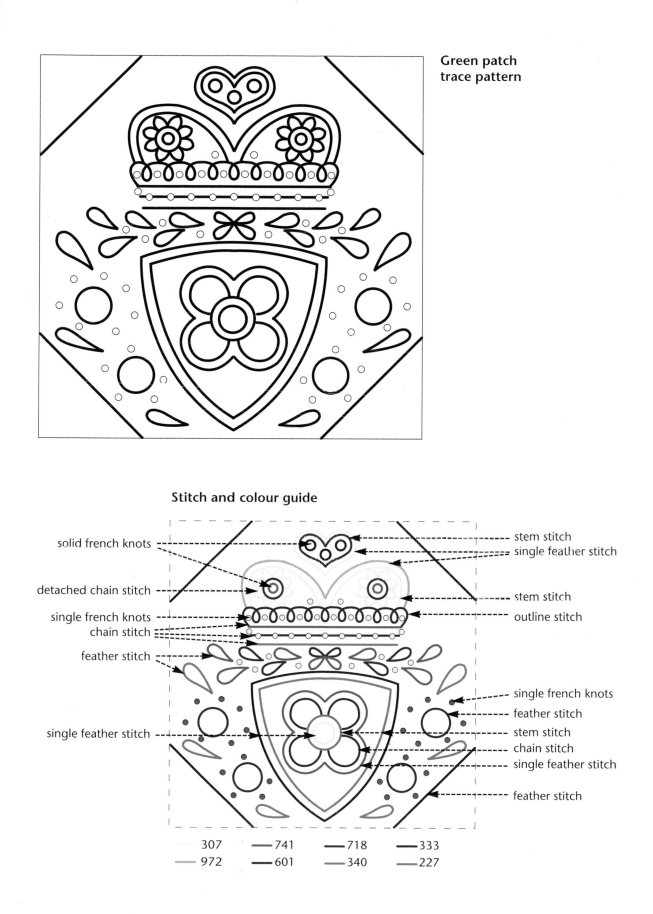

**Green patch
trace pattern**

Stitch and colour guide

solid french knots ----------→ stem stitch
----- single feather stitch

detached chain stitch ----→ stem stitch

single french knots ----→ outline stitch
chain stitch -----

feather stitch ----→

single french knots
feather stitch
single feather stitch ----→ stem stitch
chain stitch
single feather stitch

feather stitch

| | 307 | | 741 | | 718 | | 333 |
| | 972 | | 601 | | 340 | | 227 |

4
For the home

Egg cosy

◆ ◆ ◆

Perfumed drawer
sachets

◆ ◆ ◆

Small window curtain

◆ ◆ ◆

Silk tie-back

◆ ◆ ◆

House and garden
picture

EGG COSY

This little egg cosy is quickly made from a strip of cotton fabric – gathered and smocked to shape. The top of the cosy is shaped by the stitching and then secured with buttons, whereas the frill at the bottom spreads out and gives the cosy its distinctive triangular shape. Being practical as well as pretty, the cosy is softly lined to make sure the egg inside is kept as warm as toast!

Fabrics such as these, with tiny single-colour prints, make excellent backgrounds for strong contrasting smocking using single-coloured threads.

SIZE:
to fit a standard egg cup

THREADS
DMC stranded embroidery cotton:
one skein of red 350

MATERIALS
➤ 56cm x 19cm (22in x 7$\frac{1}{2}$in) of fine, printed cotton
➤ 23cm x 23cm (9in x 9in) of plain-coloured cotton for the lining
➤ One sheet of smocking dots, 6mm x 1cm ($\frac{1}{4}$in x $\frac{3}{8}$in)
➤ Sewing thread to match the fabrics
➤ Crewel needle, size 7
➤ Two contrast buttons, 1cm ($\frac{3}{8}$in) diameter

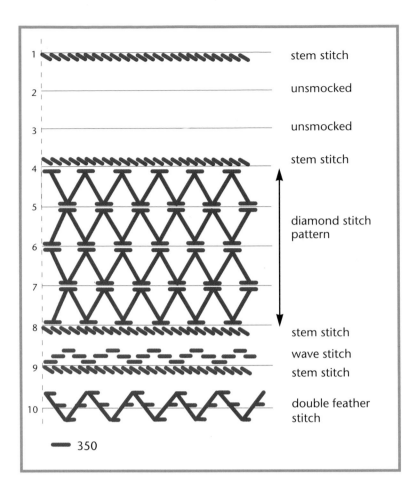

1 — stem stitch

2 — unsmocked

3 — unsmocked

4 — stem stitch

5

6 — diamond stitch pattern

7

8 — stem stitch

— wave stitch

9 — stem stitch

10 — double feather stitch

━ 350

The smocking

1 Begin by neatening the long edges of the main fabric with single turnings to the wrong side. On the top edge turn over 3.5cm (1¼in), and on the bottom edge 4cm (1½in), then pin and tack.

2 From the sheet of smocking dots, cut out 10 rows. Position them on the wrong side of the fabric so that the bottom row is 2.5cm (1in) from the edge and the top row 1.5cm (⅝in) from the edge. Pin in place, leaving 12mm (½in) seam allowances at the side edges, and press with a warm iron.

3 Gather the dots, remembering to use long lengths of sewing thread and beginning with a large knot. Pull up the threads tightly and then release them so that the gathers measure 16.5cm (6½in) between the seam allowances. Knot the ends of the threads together firmly, and even out the gathers.

4 Using three strands of thread and following the smocking chart given above left, begin the smocking on the fourth row from the top. (For how to work the smocking stitches, see page 118 onwards.) Working downwards, complete the chevron stitch diamond pattern, then the two rows of stem stitch and the band of wave stitch as shown.

Finish the bottom line of double feather stitch with a fairly loose tension; this will help the frill to stand out prettily. Work the row of stem stitch just above the diamond pattern. To shape the cosy, cut the gathering thread on the top row just above the knot and pull it up as tightly as possible, then secure the thread around a pin inserted into the seam allowance. Work stem stitch on the top row with a firm tension.

Remove the gathering threads.

Making the cosy

5 Pin the smocking right side down on your ironing board (see below), stretching the bottom edge only (along the line of double feather stitch) to about 25cm (10in). Lightly press on the wrong side.

6 At this stage, cut out the lining using the smocking as a template. Place the smocking on the lining fabric, right sides together and straight grains matching; pin and cut out.

7 Fold the smocked section in half, right sides together and seams matching. Pin and machine stitch, then press the seam open. Neaten the seam at the frill only: turn under narrow double turnings and slipstitch.

8 Stitch the lining in the same way and press open the seam. Press under a narrow turning on the lower edge, and diagonally snip around the top edge. Slip the lining over the smocked section, wrong sides together, and pin in place so that the hem just covers the lower row of smocking dots. Slipstitch in position.

9 Fold under and press a small turning on the top edge of the lining. Turn the egg cosy to the right side, place the seam to one side (this becomes the back of the cosy), and close the top simply by sewing a button onto each side.

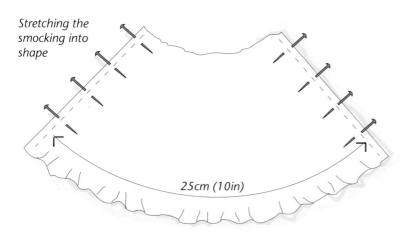

Stretching the smocking into shape

25cm (10in)

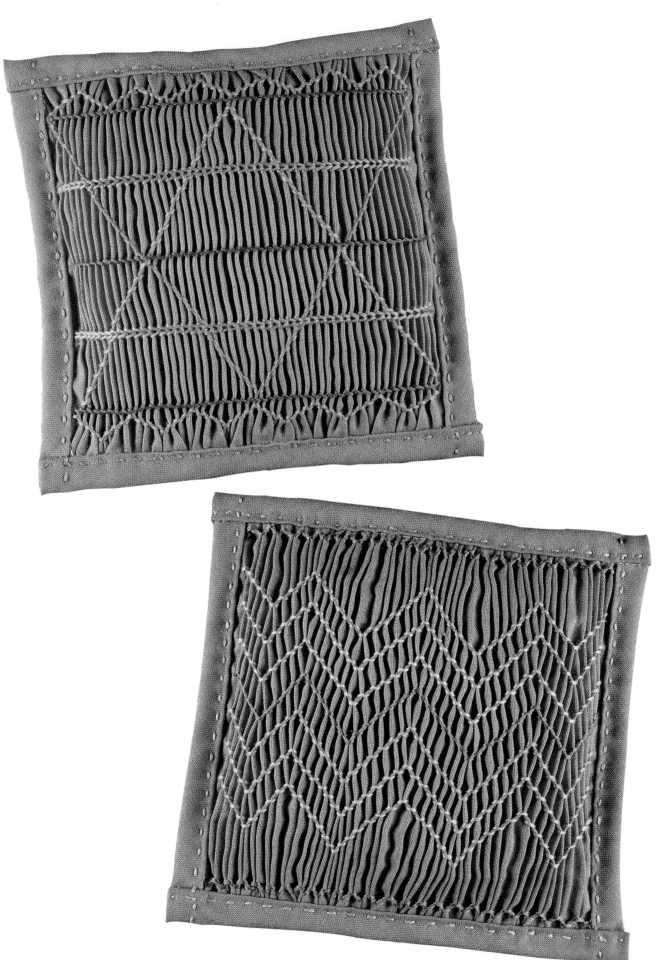

PERFUMED DRAWER SACHETS

These scented sachets came about almost by accident, as I practised a few stitches on scraps of fabric. They are so simple to make, even a beginner would be encouraged with her results.

For each sachet, an embroidered top and a plain back are simply stitched together on the right side, the scented filling is added and then the sachet is finished around the edges with matching bias binding. Alternatively, the sachets could be filled with wadding to make pretty pincushions.

SIZE:
11cm x 11cm (4¹/₂in x 4¹/₂in)

THREADS
DMC stranded embroidery cotton: one skein each of blues 3766, 964, 747, 3756; yellows 762, 742; greens 472, 280; beige 3047

MATERIALS
➤ 46cm x 46cm (18in x 18in) of deep pink cotton
➤ 46cm x 26cm (18in x 10in) of pale pink cotton
➤ Sewing thread to match the fabrics
➤ Crewel needle, size 7
➤ One sheet of smocking dots, 6mm x 1cm (¹/₄in x ³/₈in)
➤ Tracing paper, dressmaker's carbon paper
➤ Lavender or other sweet-smelling filling

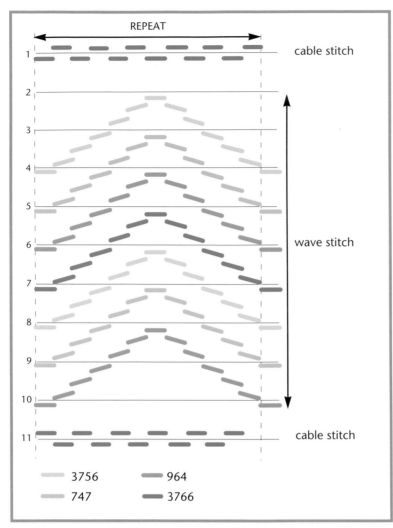

REPEAT

1 — cable stitch

2

3

4

5

6 — wave stitch

7

8

9

10

11 — cable stitch

3756   964
747   3766

Zigzag smocking chart

Cutting out the fabric

1 From the deep pink fabric, cut out two rectangles measuring 33cm x 15cm (13in x 5in) for the sachet fronts and two pieces measuring 13cm x 13cm (5in x 5in) for the sachet backs. From the remaining fabric, cut out eight bias strips, 13cm x 3cm (5in x 1¹/₄in), for binding the edges.

From the pale pink fabric, cut out two small rectangles and four bias strips to the same measurements.

The smocking

2 Cut out 11 rows of dots and apply them centrally to the wrong side of each deep pink sachet front, leaving 12mm (¹/₂in) seam allowances all round. If you are making the two smocked sachets, you could try using the same smocking dots twice, applying light pressure to the first one and heavier pressure to the second. Sometimes the second impression is still clear enough to stitch, especially on fine fabrics when very dark dots may show on the right side and spoil the effect.

3 Gather the dots, using long lengths of thread for each row. Pull the threads up in pairs, tightly at first to set the folds, then release them to measure 9cm (3¹/₂in) across. Knot the threads firmly, and even out the gathers.

4 Follow the smocking charts given above left and above right for the zigzag and diamond designs. Both designs are worked using three strands in the needle and with a light tension. For the zigzag design, work the band of wave stitch outwards from the centre, leaving the rows immediately above and below unstitched. (See pages118 onwards for instructions on how to work the stitches.) Finish rows 1 and 11 with cable stitch, then remove the gathering threads.

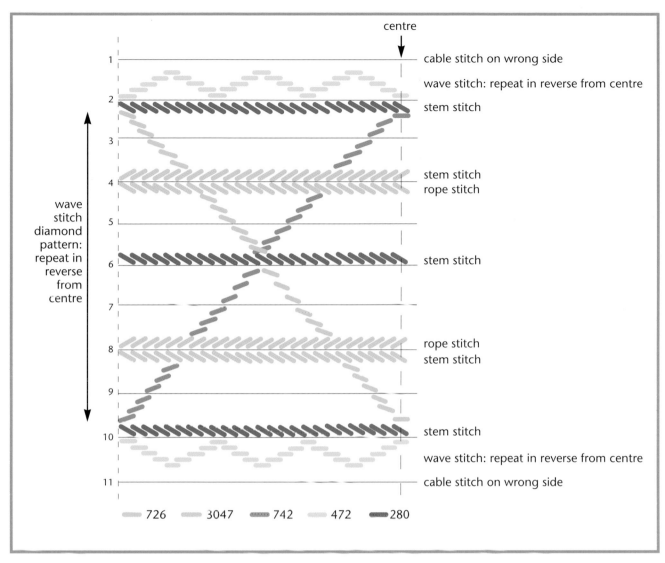

Diamond smocking chart

5 For the diamond design, above, work the rows of rope and stem stitch first, to regularize all the vertical folds. (See page 118 onwards for how to work the stitches.) Then smock the top and bottom rows of wave stitch. Finally, work the diamond pattern, slightly increasing the size of the wave stitches, in order to keep a straight line in the number of folds required. When you come to the horizontal rows, take the needle underneath and continue diagonally in pattern.

6 For both smocked sachet fronts, tack across the top and bottom seam allowances to secure the folds. Pin out and, if needed, slightly stretch the smocking to measure 10cm (4in), and press lightly on the wrong side.

The embroidery

7 For the embroidered leaf design, trace the motif given right and transfer it to the right side of the pale pink sachet front using carbon paper. (See page 137 for how to transfer designs.) Work the motif using three strands of thread throughout.

Begin the embroidery with the inside border of feather stitch and then the zigzag border in single feather stitch. (See pages 136–137 for how to work the stitches.) Next, work the centre stem (changing the stitch direction on the curves as shown) and the scrolls, also in single feather stitch. Complete the leaves with close rows of single feather stitch, and finish the leaf centres and spots in satin stitch.

Lightly steam press on the wrong side.

Making the sachets

8 All three sachets are made in the same way. Place each front and back section together, right sides outside. Pin and machine stitch around three sides. Loosely fill with lavender, pin the opening together and machine stitch across. Trim the seam allowances to 8mm (5/16in).

9 Apply strips of bias binding to each side of the sachet. Working from the back, pin and stitch strips of binding to two opposite sides, keeping the raw edges even. Fold the binding to the front; pin and tack. Repeat on the other two sides, folding in the short raw edges to neaten the corners. Hand-stitch the binding in place with running stitch and three strands of contrast thread.

Remove the tacking stitches to finish.

Leaf trace pattern

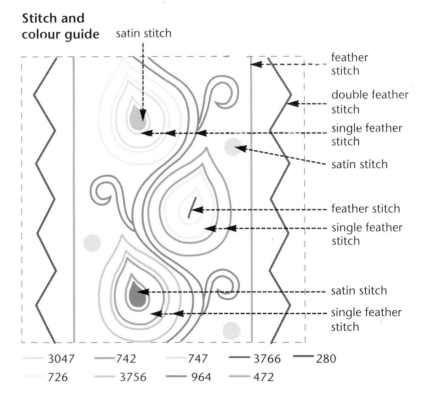

Stitch and colour guide   satin stitch

feather stitch

double feather stitch

single feather stitch

satin stitch

feather stitch

single feather stitch

satin stitch

single feather stitch

— 3047   — 742   — 747   — 3766   — 280
— 726   — 3756   — 964   — 472

SMALL WINDOW CURTAIN

Ironically, it is often the smallest windows in a home that can present a problem when it comes to choosing suitable coverings. The curtain illustrated is quick and easy to make: it provides privacy for a window which may be overlooked and, at the same time, creates a pretty style that would suit most interiors.

This simple unlined curtain has a smocked heading with a stand-up frill, and can easily be made to fit smaller or larger windows if preferred. The curtain can be hung from a narrow rod or stretch wire slotted through a fabric channel, which is neatly stitched behind the smocked heading. It is made from a washable cotton fabric with a self-coloured printed grid, so smocking dots are not required. These particular printed fabrics are often found in department stores which specialize in patchwork fabrics with small repeat patterns. Depending on the size of the window, and an average level of gathered fullness in the heading, the grid should be between 8mm–1cm ($5/16$–$3/8$in) for best results.

SIZE:
76cm x 51cm (30in x 20in)

THREAD
DMC coton à broder: one skein of white, number 16

MATERIALS
➤ 81cm x 96cm (32in x 38in) of white cotton fabric with printed grid (spots or checks)
➤ Matching sewing thread
➤ Crewel needle, size 7
➤ White tape or seam binding, 51cm x 2.5cm (20in x 1in)

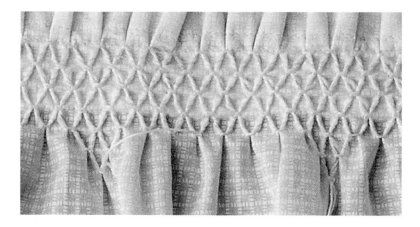

Preparing the fabric

1 Begin by turning over 4cm ($1^1/2$ in) to the wrong side on one long edge, for the frill. Pin and machine stitch, then press. Make double turnings on the side edges, turning over 5mm ($^3/16$ in) and then 1cm ($^3/8$ in). Pin and machine stitch. Turn up the hem, using a 5mm ($^3/16$ in) fold first and then 2.5cm (1in). Pin and machine stitch, as before, and press.

Curtain heading

2 On the right side, work the first row of surface honeycomb stitch across the fabric, picking up the corners of the printed (or woven) grid to form the stitch. (See page 123 for how to work surface honeycomb stitch.) Following the smocking chart given above right, work four complete rows, then finish the heading with groups of three stitches spaced equally across the bottom row, as shown on the chart.

3 The hanging threads are optional. For each group of three stitches, cut a 10cm (4in) length of coton à broder. Thread one length into the needle: take the needle under the lower stitch in the group of three and bring it back under the same stitch, leaving a small loop at the top. Unthread the needle and, with the loose ends even, thread them through the loop and pull them downwards to secure the knot. To finish, tie a knot towards the end of each loose thread. Repeat on the remaining lower stitches.

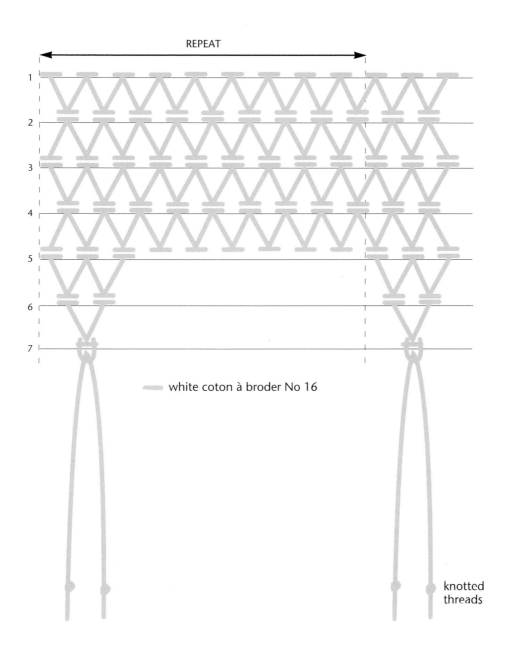

REPEAT

1

2

3

4

5

6

7

white coton à broder No 16

knotted
threads

SILK TIE-BACK

Give plain-coloured dress curtains stylish silk tie-backs, smocked and edged in bright contrasting hues for maximum effect. A simple band of smocking – with optional beaded highlights – is padded and stiffened to form a firm tie-back which will hold heavy curtains neatly in place. The basic straight tie-back has bound edges, which are ideal for covering the gathered seam allowances produced by smocking, and is held in place with brass D-rings attached to the wrong side.

SIZE:
61cm x 11cm
(24in x 4¼in)

THREADS
DMC stranded embroidery cotton: one skein each of greens 703, 701; pinks 600, 3804; purple 792

MATERIALS
➤ Dark green dupion silk: two pieces for smocking 109cm x 14.5cm (43in x 5¾in); one piece for lining 63cm x 13cm (25in x 5in)
➤ Contrast dupion silk for the binding
➤ Contrast sewing thread
➤ Matching sewing silk
➤ One sheet of (silver) smocking dots, 8mm x 10mm (⁵⁄₁₆in x ³⁄₈in)
➤ Heavyweight interfacing, 58cm x 10cm (23in x 4in)
➤ Two pieces of lightweight wadding, 58cm x 10cm (23in x 4in)
➤ Crewel needles, sizes 5 and 9
➤ Two brass D-rings
➤ Glass beads: one box each of DMC V1 04820 royal blue; V1 03702 medium leaf green; V1 04809 sky blue

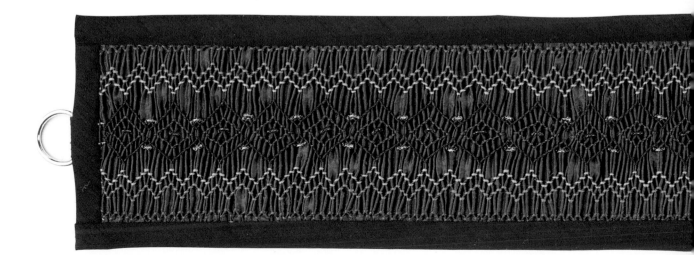

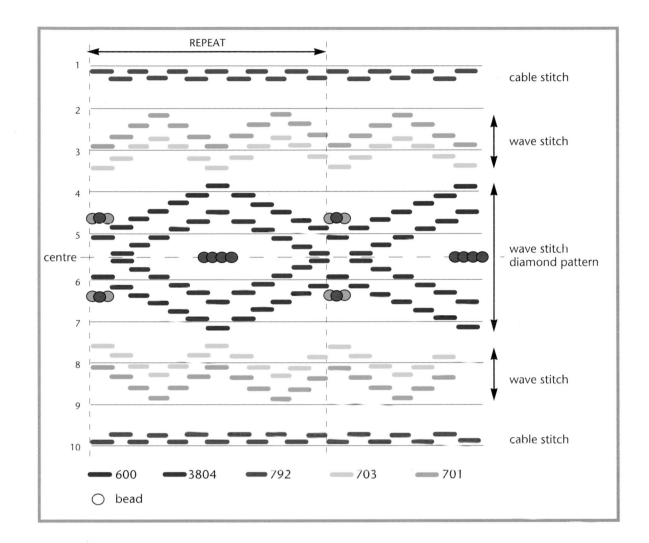

REPEAT

1 — cable stitch

2

3 — wave stitch

4

centre — wave stitch diamond pattern

5

6

7

8 — wave stitch

9

10 — cable stitch

━━ 600   ━━ 3804   ━━ 792   ━━ 703   ━━ 701

◯ bead

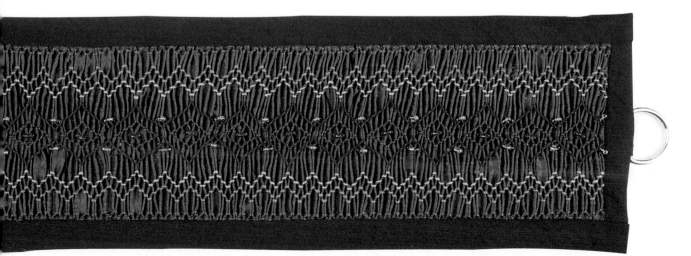

Preparing the fabric

1 With the right sides together, pin the two long pieces of silk along one short edge and machine stitch taking a 2cm (3/4in) seam. Press the seam open, and neaten the edges with zigzag stitch.

2 Cut out 10 rows of dots by 99cm (39in) twice and pin them centrally to the wrong side of the fabric, butting the short edges close together in the centre. Press with a warm dry iron.

Using the contrast sewing thread, gather the rows of dots. Pull up the threads in pairs, tightly at first to crease the folds; then release them to measure 61cm (24in).

The smocking

3 Following the smocking chart given on page 107 and using three strands in the needle, work the embroidery from the top and bottom edges towards the centre keeping an even tension. (See page 118 onwards for how to work the stitches.)

Attaching the beads

4 Using a single strand of purple 792 and the finer crewel needle, add four royal blue beads to the centre of each diamond, stitching them over the two middle folds (see below left). Take the needle to the wrong side, overstitch the two folds and bring the needle out in the next diamond. Repeat and continue in this way across the length of the smocking.

5 Then, using a single strand of green 703, attach two green beads with one sky blue bead between to the pink diamond border, as shown on the smocking chart, stitching over the two centre folds as before.

Making the tie-back

6 Remove the gathering threads and lightly press the smocking on the wrong side. Machine stitch the long edges 6mm (1/4in) away from the cable stitching to secure the folds in the seam allowances. Trim the edges back to 12mm (1/2in).

7 Place the smocking face down, lay the wadding on top and then cover with the interfacing. Pin and tack across the centre, taking large stitches through all layers.

8 From the contrast silk, cut two bias strips 66cm x 6.5cm (26in x 2 1/2in) and two others 11.5cm x 6.5cm (4 1/2in x 2 1/2in). Fold each piece in half lengthways and lightly crease the centre.

9 On the right side of the smocking, pin the two shorter lengths of (doubled) binding in position, placing the fold towards the centre and aligning it neatly with the smocking folds. Pin close to the folded edge. Fold back the top layer and tack the under layer to the smocking. Remove the pins, open out the binding and machine stitch along the creaseline.

Attaching the beads to two folds

Overcasting the two folds

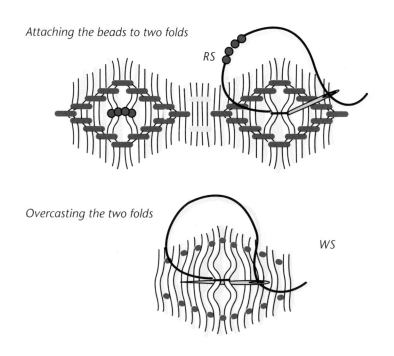

RS

WS

Fold back the top layer and tack the two edges together, trim the raw edges level with the long sides. Apply the binding to the long edges in the same way.

10 On the short edges, fold the binding to the wrong side over the 12mm (1/2in) seam allowance and catch-stitch to the interfacing. Repeat on the long edges. At the corners, take the binding straight across the short side (on the right side). Fold it back at an angle, snip into the inside fold to reduce bulk (see top right), and then turn over the top edge. This diagonal fold gives a neat finish to the edge of the corner on the wrong side (see middle right). Continue to catch-stitch the binding.

Attaching the D-rings

11 Cut two pieces of contrast fabric 5cm (2in) square. Fold in the sides to make a strip 2cm (3/4in) wide, and press. Thread on the D-ring and hand stitch across the strip (see below right).

On the wrong side of the tie-back, attach a D-ring to the centre of each short side, placing the straight side of the D just inside the bound edge. Stitch the strip first to the interfacing and then carefully through the smocking to give extra support.

The lining

12 Fold under 12mm (1/2in) turnings on all sides of the lining fabric and press. On the wrong side of the tie-back, position the second piece of wadding and then place the lining on top. Pin around the edges over the D-ring tabs.

Using matching sewing silk, slipstitch all round the edge of the lining, easing it towards the short edges. Remove the tacking stitches and ease the tie-back into a gentle curve.

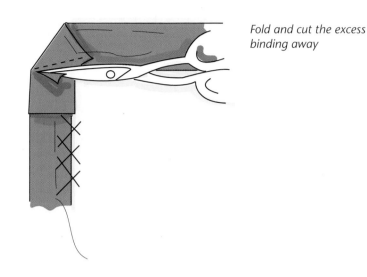

Fold and cut the excess binding away

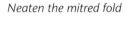

Neaten the mitred fold

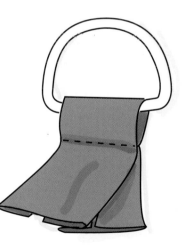

Attach the fabric tab to the D-ring

HOUSE AND GARDEN PICTURE

Double cable stitch and a lively coral background fabric combine to give this simple house and garden picture an unusual painterly effect – reminiscent of the pointillistic style of painting. If you would prefer to smock your own house and garden, or that of a friend or relative (which would make a very special present), it shouldn't be too difficult to change the details appropriately. Keep the design and colours fairly simple, and plan the design out on graph paper first; you may find it helpful to have a photograph of your chosen house for reference.

SIZE:
Mounted 25.5cm x 28cm (10in x 11in)

THREADS
DMC stranded embroidery cotton: one skein each of coral 351; red 606; pink 3804; greens 500, 907, 911, 964; blues 799, 3750; yellows 973, 742

MATERIALS
➤ 67cm x 23cm (27in x 9in) of deep coral linen/cotton mix, upholstery weight
➤ Woven check fabric, upholstery weight: two pieces 35.5cm x 13cm (14in x 5in), and two pieces 20cm x 13cm (8in x 5in)
➤ Matching and contrasting sewing thread
➤ Crewel needle, size 5
➤ One sheet smocking dots, 8mm x 13cm ($5/16$in x $1/2$in)
➤ 27cm x 25cm ($10^3/4$in x 10in) lightweight synthetic wadding
➤ 27cm x 25cm ($10^3/4$in x 10in) stiff mounting card
➤ Spray Mount or fabric glue
➤ Masking tape

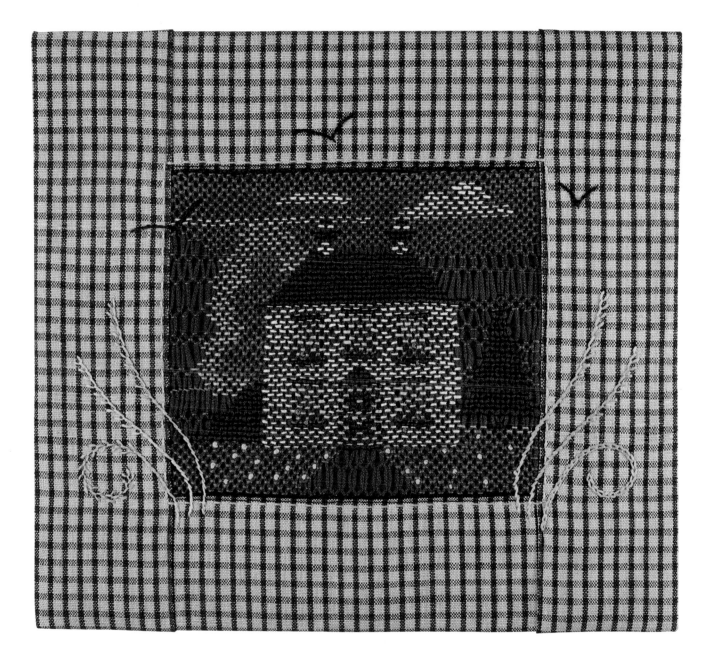

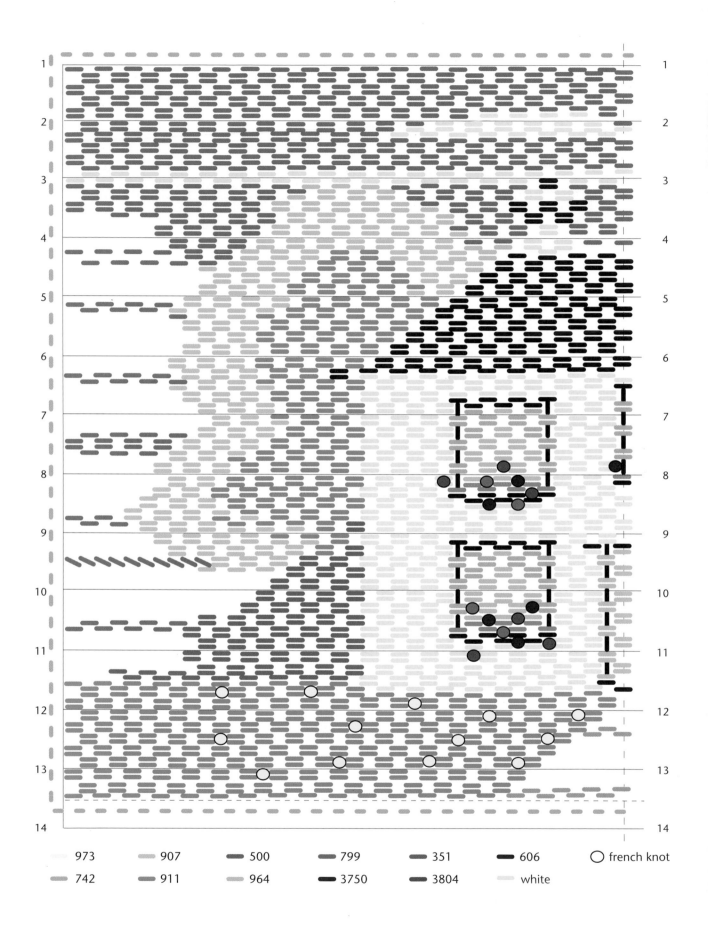

	973		907		500		799		351		606	◯ french knot
	742		911		964		3750		3804		white	

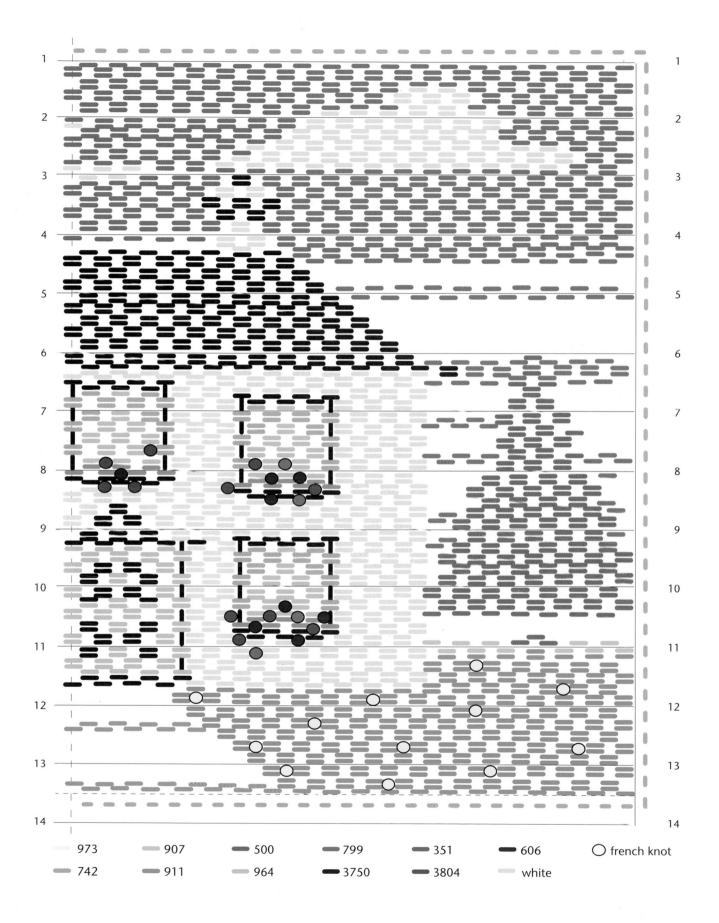

	973		907		500		799		351		606	○ french knot
	742		911		964		3750		3804		white	

Preparing the fabric

1 Neaten the raw edges of the coral fabric using machine zigzag stitch, or overcast it by hand. Cut out 14 rows of dots, 61cm (24in) across, and apply them centrally to the wrong side of the fabric using a warm, dry iron.

The smocking

2 Using long lengths of the contrast sewing thread, with a large knot at the end of each length, pick up the rows of dots. Working with the threads in pairs, pull up the gathers very tightly to crease the fabric folds and then release them to measure 18cm (7in). Knot the threads firmly and even out the gathers, stroking the fabric folds with a needle.

The smocking diagram given on pages 112 and 113 shows the house and garden scene in colour and, because it is worked completely in cable stitch, each row of stitching is marked between the black lines of the gathering threads for your guidance. Note that all the flowers in the lawn and window boxes are french knots worked on top of the finished smocking. (See page 118 onwards for how to work the stitches.) The sides of the windows and the door are suggested by threading dark blue thread under the finished cable stitching.

3 Following the smocking diagram and working with three strands in the needle, begin at the top with the sky. On the third row down, work one or two rows of the white cloud – this should be quite easy as you have now established the size of your stitch, and you can turn your embroidery upside down to work the reverse rows.

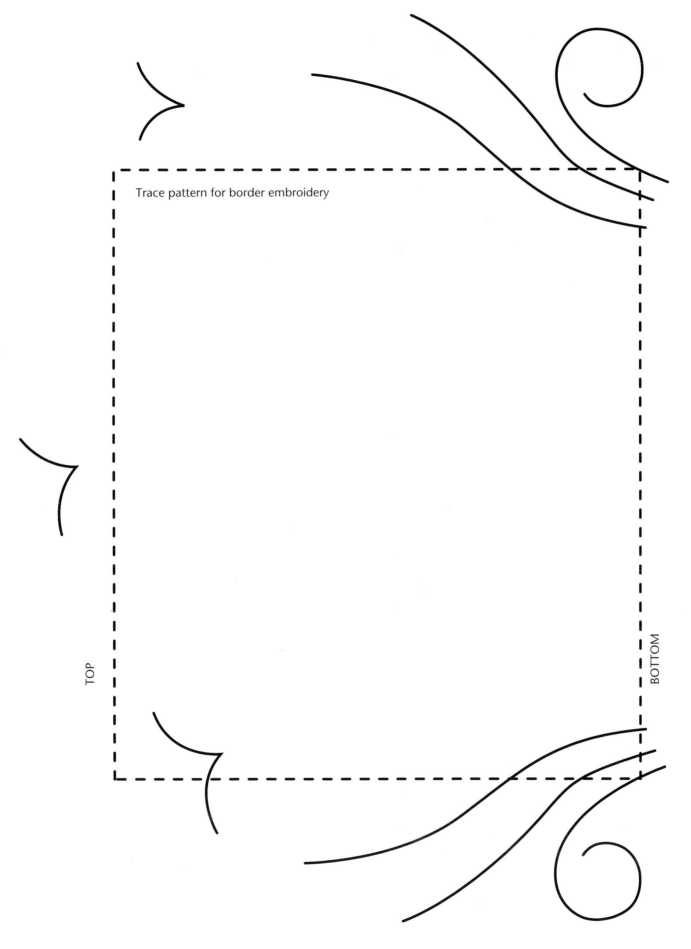

Trace pattern for border embroidery

TOP

BOTTOM

Don't work too many rows of the cloud before completing more of the sky. The idea is to keep all the rows evenly horizontal, otherwise the effect may look messy rather than pleasantly pointillistic.

4 Working downwards, begin the trees to the left of the house and then work the roof. Continue to work the trees perhaps as far as the next row of gathering threads. Then begin the house, carefully working the first two rows in white and then the tops of the windows in darker blue.

5 I then worked the yellow curtains and levelled the house in white before working the turquoise window panes. This was followed by more house in white and the windowsills.

6 Continue in this way, working the house and then completing the door. Finish each side of the door, working the windows and the house as before. Complete the trees to the left of the house.

7 To keep the unstitched gathers even at each side of the house, work cable stitch in coral on the wrong side along the gathered rows. Work the sky lines in blue and the fir tree.

8 Complete the smocking by working the lawn and the drive.

9 Add the lines at the sides of the windows and door. Using six strands of thread, work the french knots.

10 To give depth to the scene, work single rows of 3750 dark blue stem stitch at the top and bottom of the picture.

11 Remove the gathering threads and lightly press the embroidery on the wrong side, pinning it to measure 16cm x 14cm (6$\frac{1}{4}$in x 5$\frac{1}{2}$in). Trim the seam allowances to 2cm ($\frac{3}{4}$in).

Adding the fabric border

12 On the two shorter lengths of checked border fabric, turn under 2cm ($^3/_4$in) on one long side and tack. Place them on the right side of the picture, with the folded edge next to the blue lines at the top and bottom. Pin, tack and machine stitch close to the fold. Turn under the long border pieces and apply them to the sides of the picture in the same way. Remove the tacking stitches. Using four strands of yellow 724, work a row of running stitches around the border close to the machine stitching.

13 Transfer the birds and grass motifs on page 115 to the border using carbon paper and pencil. (I used bright red carbon paper.) Using four strands of blue 3750, embroider the birds in rope stitch. Work the tall grasses using yellow 973 and green 907 in single feather and stem stitch; and finally the curled stems using green 907 in chain stitch and feather stitch. Remove any tacking stitches and press lightly on the wrong side with a steam iron or under a damp cloth.

Mount the picture, securing the corners with masking tape

Fold the fabric over; first on one side, then on the opposite side

Mounting the picture

14 Embroidered pictures tend to look best if they are first stretched over cardboard before being framed under glass. The size of the cardboard includes 6mm ($^1/_4$in) all round to allow for the recess in a picture frame.

Begin by covering one side of the cardboard with Spray Mount. Position the wadding in the centre of the cardboard and press it in place.

15 On the right side of the embroidery, mark the outer edge of the border with pins. Lay it face down, and centre the cardboard on top, wadding side down and aligning the edges with the pins.

16 Following the diagrams above, fold over the fabric at each corner and secure it with pieces of masking tape. Working first on one side and then on the opposite side, fold the fabric over on all edges, holding it firmly with masking tape (see above).

Remove the pins. If you are using a checked fabric, use the straight lines of the checks as a guide.

17 Check to see if the picture is central and adjust the masking tape if necessary. Neaten the corners with a mitred fold, smoothing the fabric evenly and securing it with more tape. Overstitch the mitred seam for a neat finish.

STITCH LIBRARY
Smocking Stitches

Smocking stitches form a special type of embroidery that is used solely to decorate and secure the gathered folds of smocking. There are several basic stitches that can be worked either on their own, or combined with others to make narrow bands or deeper all-over patterns, in single or mixed colours.

Each stitch produces a certain amount of elasticity – some, such as stem stitch, give firm control to the folds, while others, such as the diamond pattern, are very elastic – a point to be aware of when choosing your own stitches.

The following instructions include all the smocking stitches used to make the projects in the book.

STEM AND ROPE STITCHES

Stem and rope stitches give firm control to the smocking gathers and are often worked in conjunction with each other – either as two rows worked closely together to give a plaited effect, or spaced further apart to add firm tension throughout the smocking. Note that stem stitch slants downwards and rope stitch slants upwards.

Stem stitch

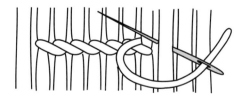

Bring the needle up through the first fold on the left. With the thread below the needle, and working from left to right, work stem stitch across the row, taking a small stitch through the top of each fold. Complete the row, keeping the stitches a uniform length and the tension even.

Rope stitch

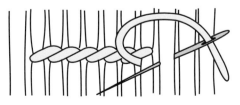

Bring the needle up beside the first fold on the left. With the thread above the needle and working from left to right, work rope stitch across the row, taking a small stitch through the top of each fold. Complete the row, keeping the stitches and tension even.

CABLE STITCHES

A single line of cable stitch gives firm control to the smocking. Although this is not quite as much as a single line of stem or rope, it gives a pretty stepped effect with a softer edge, which you may prefer. Cable stitches can be worked as single or double rows or combined with other stitches to make all-over patterns.

Cable stitch

Bring the needle up beside the first fold on the left. Working from left to right and with the thread above the needle, make a small stitch through the top of the next fold, as for rope stitch. Then with the thread below the needle, make a small stitch through the next fold, as for stem stitch. Continue in this way across the row, working each stitch alternately with the thread above and below the needle.

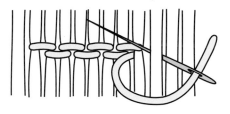

Double cable stitch

Work the first row following the instructions given for cable stitch (above). Working from left to right, as before, bring out the needle beside the same fold where you began the previous row, but slightly lower down. With the thread below the needle, make a small stitch through the next fold, and then continue working the stitches as before. Note that the stitches of the second row are placed in the reverse position from those in the first, to give this attractive brick effect.

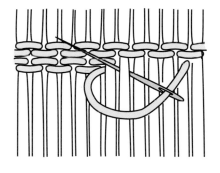

Cable trellis pattern

This combination of stitches, with its very pretty trellis pattern, gives a fairly elastic finish to the smocking, and looks best worked on larger panels rather than on narrow borders.

1 Working from left to right, bring the needle up to the left of the fold on row one. Make three cable stitches, beginning with the thread above the needle. Then take the needle down to row two and make a single backstitch over the next fold with the thread above the needle. Make three cable stitches as before, then take the needle up to row one and work another single backstitch with the thread below the needle. Repeat this sequence across the row.

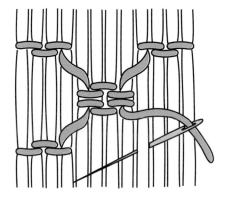

1

2 Working from left to right, bring up the needle to the left of the fold on row three. Make three cable stitches, beginning with the thread below the needle, then continue along the row, working the stitches in reverse pattern as shown. Repeat these three rows to give the diamond trellis effect.

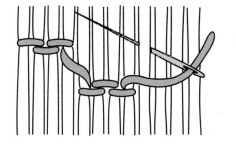

2

1

2

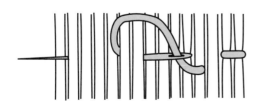

CHEVRON STITCHES

Chevron stitch gives great elasticity to the smocking. It can be worked as a single row, perhaps near a frill to release the fullness of the gathered fabric, or as several rows repeated in a zigzag pattern across the area to be smocked or as the ever-popular diamond stitch pattern.

1 Bring the needle out to the left of the first fold on row two. Take it up to row one and, with the thread below the needle, backstitch over the second fold. With the thread above the needle, backstitch over the third fold, bringing the needle out in the centre of the two folds, pulling them together.

2 Take the needle down to row two and, with the thread above the needle, backstitch the fourth fold. With the thread below the needle, backstitch over the fifth fold, bringing the needle out in the centre of the two folds as before. Repeat the sequence from the beginning and continue to the end of the row.

Diamond stitch pattern

This pretty all-over diamond pattern gives a very elastic finish to the smocking. It is formed by working two rows of chevron stitch in reverse to each other and repeating them in sequence over the area whicb is going to be smocked.

Work the first row as described for chevron stitch, placing the stitches just inside the rows. Working from left to right, bring the needle out to the left of the fold on row two, just below the previously made stitch. Complete the chevron stitch in reverse so that the second chevron forms the first diamond shape. Note that the two stitches in the middle of the diamond share the same row, so in each case, they should be placed just inside the row. Continue to the end of the row and repeat as required.

BACKSTITCH

Backstitch used in smocking (as on the baby's drawstring bag) is combined with other firm control stitches. It is used to soften the edges of a smocked panel, where every other pair of folds is backstitched.

Working from right to left, bring the needle out to the left of the first pair of folds. Backstitch over the two folds, inserting the needle to the right, and bringing it up again to the left of the next pair of folds to be secured. Repeat the stitch across the row.

WAVE STITCHES

Worked as a single row, wave stitch gives medium control to the smocking and, for every additional row, the control is slightly increased. This is a very versatile stitch that can be worked in different multiples of stitches to give greater or smaller 'waves'. It can be repeated in two or three rows to make a solid border, or worked in reverse to form diamonds.

Wave stitch

Working from left to right, bring the thread out to the left of the first fold. With the thread above the needle, backstitch the second fold, slightly angling the needle downwards. Continue to work three more stitches (or the required number) in a diagonal line, and on the fourth stitch place the thread below the needle. Work the same number of stitches upwards, angling the needle upwards. Repeat the 'waves' across the the row.

Long wave stitch

By working wave stitch with the needle at a greater angle and with longer than normal stitches, interesting two-tone effects are created – much like a twisted cord. The stitch is particularly good for smocking linear designs, as in the girl's bag, and is very quickly worked.

1 Bring the needle out to the left of the first fold. With the thread below the needle and making a diagonal stitch upwards, insert the needle over the second fold. Keeping the needle at an angle, bring it out the same distance above. Make the next stitch in the same way over the third fold and so on.

2 At the top of the 'wave' place the thread above the needle and work in reverse, angling the needle and stitches downwards. For very long lines, be guided by how many slanting stitches fit comfortably between two rows, and then repeat them to give a neat finish.

Double wave pattern

This stitch gives medium control to the smocking gathers. For greater control, several rows of wave stitch can be worked close together in either plain or mixed colours.

Work the first row as described for wave stitch. Working from left to right, bring the needle out just below the first stitch. Continue to work the second row of wave stitch, keeping the two rows close together, the stitches a uniform length and the tension even.

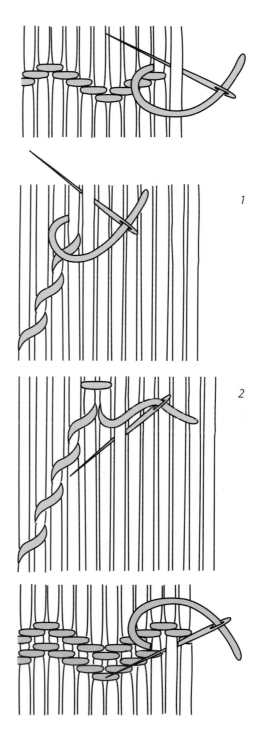

1

2

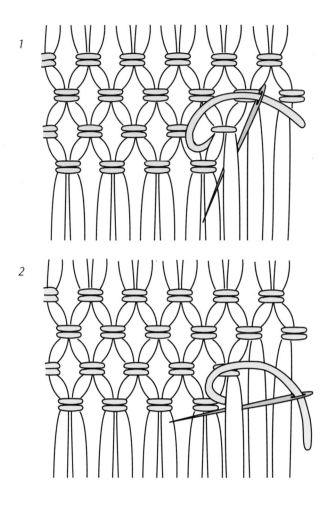

HONEYCOMB STITCHES

These stitches draw the gathered folds into a very attractive honeycomb pattern, and give great elasticity to the smocking.

Honeycomb stitch

1 Working from left to right, bring the needle out to the left of the fold and backstitch the first two folds twice, pulling them together. Slip the needle behind the fold and bring it out to the left of the second fold on the row below.

2 Backstitch the second and the third folds together twice. Pass the needle behind and bring it out to the left of the third fold on row one. Stitch the third and fourth folds together as before. Repeat the sequence from the beginning and complete the row. Work the next and subsequent rows in the same way.

Honeycomb stitch on multicoloured checks

The beauty of using woven checks, instead of transferred dots, is that the smocking is so much quicker to work – and the gathered checks make additional interesting patterns.

Work in a similar way as described for honeycomb stitch above, but instead of working on pre-gathered folds, pick up the corners of the checks, and work from right to left.

Bring the needle out at the top right-hand corner of the first multicoloured check to be smocked, a stitch length inside the smaller square A as shown in the diagram. Working from right to left, make a small stitch and bring the needle out.

Make a small stitch in the corner of square B to the left, pulling the two stitches together. Then make a small stitch over the two folds, bringing the needle out directly below, in the lower corner of square C.

Repeat as for step one and, after over-stitching the two folds C and D together, take the needle back to the top of the multicoloured check; continue to the end of the row, repeating the two stages as you go.

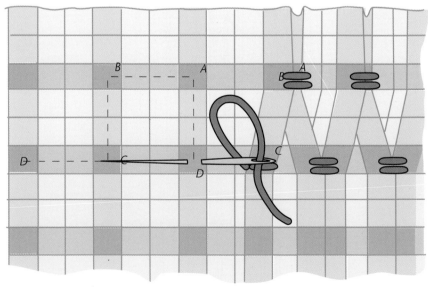

Surface honeycomb stitch

A pretty textured stitch, where the embroidery thread lies on the surface of the fabric folds in honeycomb pattern; this stitch gives medium elasticity to the smocking.

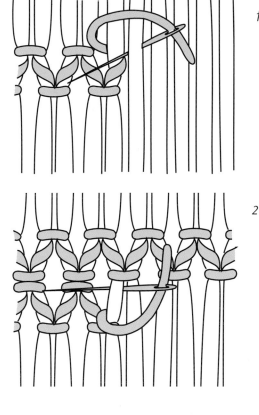

1 Working from left to right, bring the needle out to the left of the first fold. With the thread above the needle, backstitch the first and second folds. Bring the needle out in the centre of the two folds, pulling them together.

With the thread above the needle, make a similar stitch over the same fold but on the row below, and continue to work along the row in the same way.

2 With the thread below the needle, backstitch the second and third folds together, bringing the needle out in the centre of the folds as before. Keeping the thread below the needle, backstitch the third fold on the row above. Backstitch the third and fourth folds together with the thread above the needle. Repeat these two steps to the end of the row, and work subsequent rows in the same way.

DOUBLE FEATHER STITCH

To work double feather stitch on gathers, position the fabric so that the folds are running horizontally across the work. Bring the needle out in the centre of where you plan to work the feather stitch border.

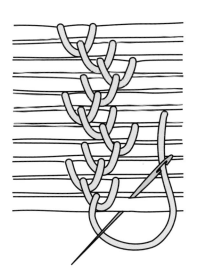

Working downwards, and with the thread under the left thumb, make a stitch to the right, picking up the top of the fabric fold. With the thread still below and working downwards, work two more stitches to the right, as for surface double feather stitch. Now work two feather stitches to the left. Repeat the sequence and continue to the end of the row.

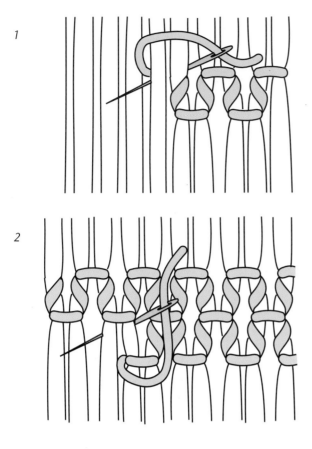

VANDYKE STITCHES

These stitches are very similar to surface honeycomb stitch, and produce the same amount of elasticity, but the threads make a slightly different pattern on the surface of the folds.

Vandyke stitch

1 Working from right to left, bring the needle up beside the second fold. With the thread above the needle, backstitch the first and second folds, pulling them together. Continue in this way, working alternately up and down to the end of the row.

2 To complete the diamond effect on the next and subsequent rows, simply pass the needle behind the stitch on the top row and then work the usual backstitch on the row below.

Vandyke stitch on tartan

This may look daunting, but once you have worked out your own grid, the smocking is no more difficult than on plain fabric. The illustration shows how the plain areas have been divided into similar-sized checks as those produced by the tartan stripes. You may find it easier to mark the first plain area with a grid of pencil dots.

Working from right to left, proceed as for Vandyke stitch (above), picking up the appropriate 'corners' of the rectangles made where the tartan stripes cross (1), and your pencil dots in the plain areas (2). Keep the stitches even throughout.

After working one or two plain areas with dots, you will soon get used to the number of stitches to work. Continue to the end of the row, and repeat as required.

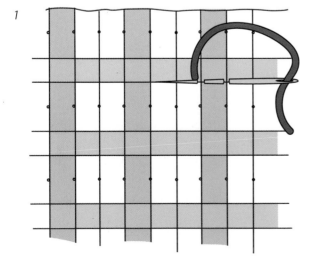

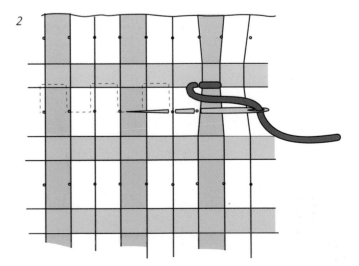

STITCH LIBRARY
Embroidery Stitches

A variety of embroidery stitches are often added to smocking for texture and simple decoration. They can be worked between rows of smocking, around the edges of smocked panels, or within trellis patterns, for example.

Complementary panels of embroidery and smocking can also be combined with colourful results, as in the nine-patch cushion on page 80.

Instructions for working the embroidery stitches used in the projects are given in the following pages.

Stem stitch

Stem stitch is essentially an outlining stitch, but is frequently used to suggest the stems of flowers and leaves in floral designs.

Bring out the needle on the stitchline and, working from left to right, make a stitch along the stitchline to the right. Bring the needle out half a stitch length back, with the thread looped to the left and below the needle, ready to make the next stitch. Repeat the sequence, making evenly spaced stitches.

For a broader stem stitch, work as before but angle the stitch slightly where the needle enters and emerges from the fabric.

Outline stitch

This stitch is used mainly in tandem with stem stitch specifically for curved lines, where it is worked in a similar way. Note that stem stitch will naturally make a concave line whereas outline stitch will naturally make a (reverse) convex line.

Bring the needle out on the stitchline and, working from left to right, make a stitch to the right with the thread looped to the left and above the stitchline. Bring the needle out half a stitch length back, ready to make the next stitch in the same way.

Repeat, making evenly spaced stitches. Should the curve change direction, simply place the thread below the stitchline and continue with stem stitch, and vice versa.

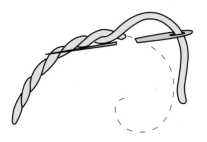

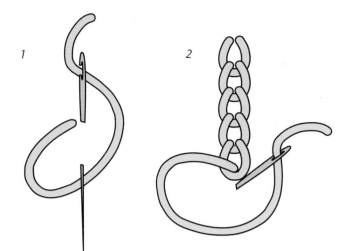

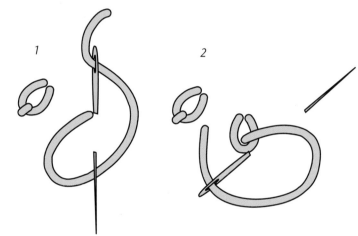

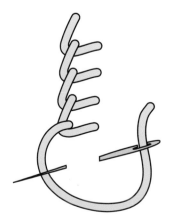

CHAIN STITCH

This is a very popular outlining stitch which, as its name implies, gives the appearance of the links in a chain. Each stitch is made by forming a loop with the thread, which is taken under the needle point before the stitch is pulled to shape.

1 Bring the needle out at the beginning of the stitchline. Working downwards, and holding the thread down with the left thumb, a little to the left, insert the needle at the starting point to form a loop. Bring the needle out a short distance below, with the thread under the needle.

2 Continue in this way to the end of the row, always inserting the needle into the hole made by the emerging thread. At the end of the row, take a small stitch over the last chain loop to hold it down.

SINGLE CHAIN STITCH

This stitch is a single unattached stitch, often worked in groups or circles to suggest leaves and flowers.

1 Bring the needle out at the place to be stitched. Make a chain loop exactly as for chain stitch, bringing the needle out at the required length of the stitch.

2 Make a small tying-down stitch, ensuring that the needle is inserted just outside the loop and, in the same movement, bringing it out again at the next place to be stitched.

FEATHER STITCHES

The following group of feather stitches were all used originally to decorate nineteenth century smocks, largely to embellish the flat fabric panels at either side of the smocking but also as a means of securing the gathers. Their names derive from the featherlike effects of working open looped stitches alternately to the left and right of a central point.

You may also have seen the basic feather stitches in crazy patchwork and appliqué, where they are stitched over adjoining seams, usually in very bright colours. The stitches illustrated below are for working on flat fabric; see page 123 for working feather stitches on smocking.

Single feather stitch

Bring the needle out on the stitchline. Working downwards from top to bottom and holding the thread under the left thumb, insert the needle a short distance to the right in a slanting direction. Bring it out on the stitchline below, and repeat to the end of the row.

Feather stitch

1 Bring the needle out on the stitchline. Working downwards, and holding the thread under the left thumb, insert the needle a short distance to the right on the same level. Make a short diagonal stitch back towards the stitchline, and bring the needle out with the thread below.

2 Now insert the needle a short distance to the left, level with the point where the thread last emerged. Make a short diagonal stitch downwards and bring it out near the stitchline with the thread below the needle, as before. Repeat these two stitches in sequence to the end of the row.

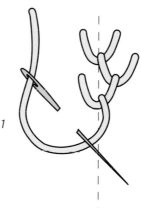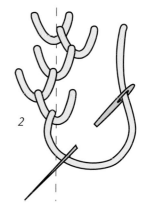

Double feather stitch

This stitch makes a very pretty zigzag border – and is generally favoured for its light, feathery look. Instead of working single stitches alternately left and right (as in feather stitch), two stitches are made consecutively to one side and then the other. To keep the even appearance of the zigzag, the first stitch is made in the opposite direction (because it is one of the previous pair of stitches) as shown below.

1 Bring the needle out on the stitchline (the centre of the border being stitched). Working downwards and with the thread under the left thumb, make one stitch to the right, as for feather stitch, and then make two stitches to the left, bringing the needle out with the thread under the needle, as before.

2 To complete the zigzag, make two stitches to the right in the same way. Repeat the sequence and continue to the end of the row.

RUNNING STITCH

This is used in embroidery primarily as a very easy-to-do outline stitch, but it is also an effective stitch for securing hems on embroidered items, using decorative threads. The stitches may be the same length on each side or slightly longer on the front.

Working from right to left, bring the needle out on the stitchline and make a short stitch to the left, bringing it up again an equal distance away. Continue to the end of the row, picking up several stitches on the needle before pulling it through.

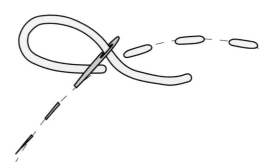

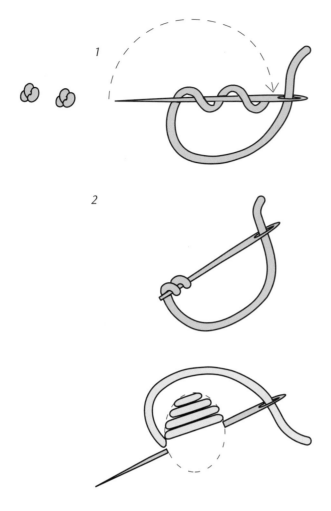

FRENCH KNOT

Knots used in embroidery, either singly or in clusters, give a raised effect and a wonderful tactile quality which combines beautifully with the gathered folds of smocking.

1 Bring the thread out at the required position and hold it firmly with the left thumb and first finger, a short distance to the left. Now twist the needle two or three times around the taut thread and insert it in the fabric, close to the starting point.

2 Keeping your left thumb over the knot, pull the thread through to the back, tightening the knot. In a separate movement, bring the needle to the front ready to make the next stitch.

SATIN STITCH

Satin stitch is a solid filling stitch often used to fill areas such as flower petals and leaves. As its name suggests, it gives a smooth, silky finish to the filled area, and reflects the light very prettily, the exact effect depending on the direction in which the stitch is made.

Bring the needle out to the left of the area to be filled. Make a slanting stitch upwards to the right and bring the needle out below, close to the starting point. Continue to work straight diagonal stitches close together until the area is filled, being careful to keep the outline edges even.

STITCH LIBRARY
Bead Embroidery

The application of beads to embroidery, either singly or in more solid patterns, offers tremendous scope for adding twinkling highlights. In some cases, the additional weight of more solid glass beadwork combined with its coldness of touch, can simply transform ordinary embroidery into something quite special.

APPLYING SINGLE BEADS

1 Bring the needle out in the place you plan to stitch the bead. Thread the bead onto the needle, slide it along the sewing thread, then make a small stitch, inserting the needle into the same hole as that of the emerging thread. Making the stitch slightly longer than the bead, pull the needle through with the thread below the point.

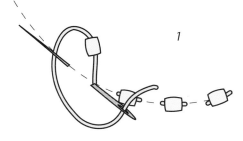

2 Take the needle to the wrong side, inserting it over the thread to secure the bead firmly to the fabric, and bring it out ready to attach the next bead.

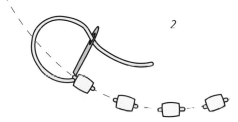

ATTACHING ONE BEAD BEHIND ANOTHER

This technique has been used on the frill of the confetti flute, page 30, where both sides are decorated with beads.

Working from the right side, apply the first bead as described above. Take the needle to the back, apply a second bead over the first stitching and then slip the needle between the layers to bring it up on the right side, ready to attach the first bead of the next pair.

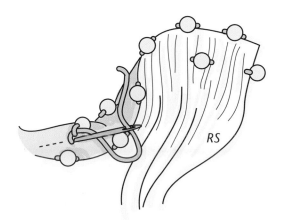

SEWING EQUIPMENT AND SKILLS

The equipment and skills required for making the projects in the book are both minimal. However, having the right tools to hand at the beginning of a job will contribute enormously to the efficiency and success of your finished projects. Given below is a checklist of very basic equipment for your work basket, and illustrated in the following pages are all the sewing skills you will need to complete your smocking with pleasing results.

Sewing Equipment

Pins:
3cm (1¼in) long stainless steel are easier to handle than short ones

Sewing needles:
mixed sizes

Sewing thread:
pure silk, cotton, cotton/polyester for hand and machine sewing

Tacking cotton:
softly twisted cotton, which breaks easily for removal, and does not leave marks on the fabric when pressed with the iron

Thimble:
for hand sewing bulky seams

Scissors:
dressmaker's shears for cutting out fabric; embroidery scissors for snipping into seams and trimming threads; general-purpose scissors for cutting cords and paper

Tape measure

Ruler and pencil

Ribbon threader

Bodkin

Rouleau turner or handle of knitting needle

Fabric adhesive

Dressmaker's carbon paper

Tracing paper

In addition to the equipment for your work basket, a sewing machine is useful for making up items, especially where long seams are involved. It need not be a highly complicated machine, as long as it can produce a good straight line and has a swing needle for zigzag stitch (for neatening seams) and a zipper foot for applying zips. Otherwise, all these operations can be done by hand, but they will take a little longer.

A steam iron (or dry iron and damp cloth) and ironing board are essential for a good finish.

Sewing Skills

TACKING

Tacking is a temporary stitch used to hold together two or more layers of fabric, usually before machine stitching. Using tacking cotton and beginning with a knot, make even length stitches about 6mm (^{1}/4in) apart, working just inside the seamline.

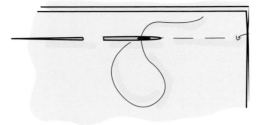

PLAIN SEAM

Most items in the book are made with plain seams, which may be straight or curved. The edges of curved seams may need to be snipped before turning through, so that the seam allowances will lie flat.

1 For a plain seam, pin the two pieces of fabric right sides together, raw edges even. Stitch a line of tacking just inside the seamline.

2 Adjust the stitch length to suit the fabric, and stitch on the seamline, neatening the sewing threads at each end by working two or three reverse stitches.

3 Place the fabric on the ironing board, and steam press the seam to sink the stitches into the fabric.

4 Now press the seam allowance open. To remove any marks which may show on the right side, press under the raw edges with the point of the iron.

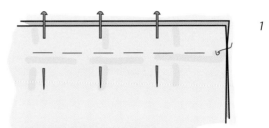

1

2

3

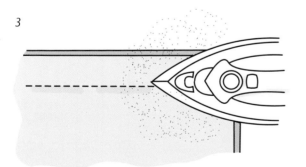

4

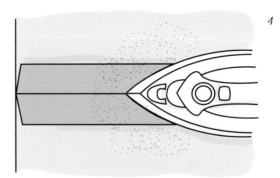

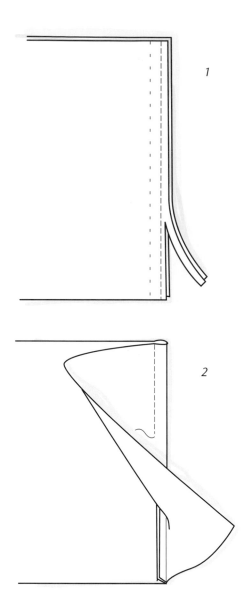

1

2

FRENCH SEAM

This is a concealed seam – stitched once from the right side and once from the wrong side – and best for narrow seams, 6mm ($^1/_4$in) wide or smaller, on lightweight fabrics.

1 Pin the two pieces of fabric wrong sides together and stitch a 1cm ($^3/_8$in) seam. Trim the allowance to 3mm ($^1/_8$in), and press the seam open.

2 With the right sides together and the stitchline on the folded edge, press the seam. Pin and stitch 6mm ($^1/_4$in) from the edge; press the seam to one side.

ZIGZAG STITCH

If your sewing machine has a swing needle, neaten the raw edges on fabrics that fray easily with a medium zigzag stitch. Stitch near, but not on, the edge of the fabric, and trim close to the stitching (below left).

HAND OVERCASTING

Overcast stitch is used to neaten raw edges, particularly on seam allowances but also on the edges of fabrics that fray easily, such as silks and satins, while being embroidered in the hand. The size of the stitching depends on the thickness of the fabric, but the stitches will normally be about 3mm ($^1/_8$in) deep and 5mm ($^3/_{16}$in) apart (below right). Overcast with an even tension, otherwise the edge may curl.

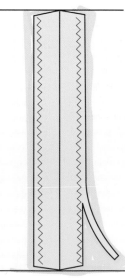

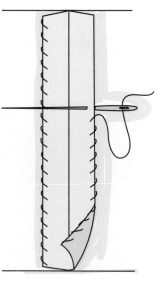

SQUARE CUSHION COVER

The simplest cover for a square cushion consists of two squares of fabric (top and bottom), which are stitched together around the edges, leaving an opening for inserting the pad. The pad should be about 2.5cm (1in) bigger than the cover to give a well-plumped, snug fit, and the opening is closed with slipstitch.

1 Cut out the front and back sections of fabric on the straight grain, adding appropriate seam allowances. Pin and tack the two pieces right sides together, stitching just inside the seamline. Stitch on the seamline, and across the corners for one or two stitches to soften the line. Leave an opening in the centre of one side.

2 Trim across the corners to reduce the bulk when it is turned right side out. Neaten the seams as appropriate.

3 Remove the tacking stitches, and turn the cover through to the right side. Ease the corners out using the round end of a knitting needle. Turn under and tack the seam allowances of the opening, and press if needed.

4 Insert the cushion pad, distributing the filling evenly. Using matching sewing thread, slipstitch the opening closed. Remove the tacking stitches.

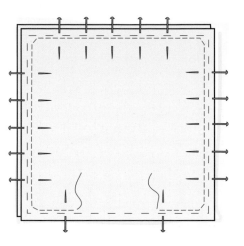

1

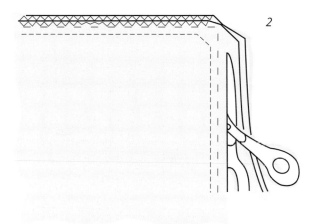

2

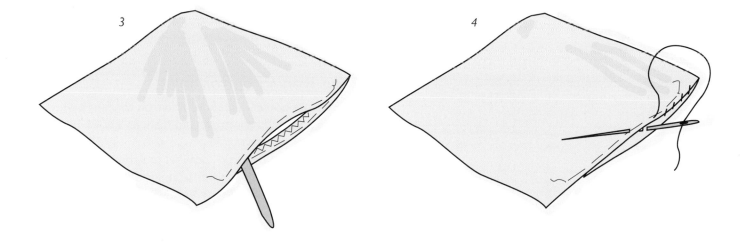

3

4

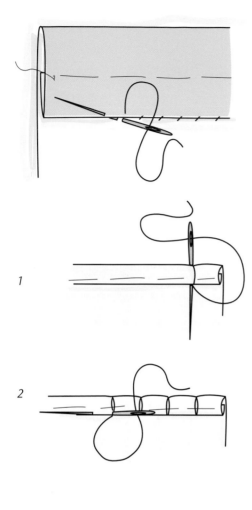

HEMMING STITCH

This is used to secure all types of hems and for finishing bound edges. Fold the hem or binding to the wrong side, pin or tack. Holding the needle at a slight angle, make a tiny stitch in the fabric and then, taking it forward a short distance, make a small stitch in the hem fold. Bring the needle out and continue in this way along the hem.

SHELL HEMMING

This pretty edging stitch is best on narrow hems of lightweight fabrics.

1 First make a double hem to the wrong side of the fabric, about 6mm (^{1}/4in) wide; pin and tack. Using matching or contrast sewing thread, bring the needle out just below the hem. Make two oversewing stitches in the same place, pulling tightly to gather the hem.

2 Pass the needle through the hem, about 1cm (^{3}/8in), and bring it out ready to repeat the two oversewing stitches, and to complete the first shell. Repeat along the hem as necessary.

BUTTONS AND BUTTONHOLES

For this type of closure, first choose the buttons, and calculate the length of the buttonholes required – this should equal the diameter plus the depth of the button. Then work the buttonholes before attaching the buttons.

Hand-worked buttonholes

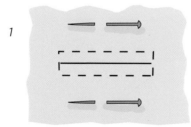

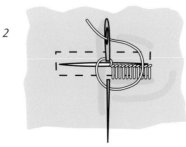

Mark the position of each buttonhole on the fabric with pins. Then draw the centre line to mark its length, but do not cut at this stage.

1 Secure the fabric layers together at either side of the buttonhole with pins. Work running stitch around the mark, about 2mm (^{1}/10in) away from it.

2 Cut along the centre line using sharp-pointed embroidery scissors. Check that the button will pass through. Secure the thread on the wrong side and, working from right to left, insert the needle from behind the slit, pointing downwards, and bring it out just below the running stitches. Pass the thread around the point of the needle from left to right, and pull the needle through, placing the purl edge of the stitch on the cut fabric edge.

3 Complete one side of the buttonhole, then fan out the stitches around the end nearest to the garment edge. Buttonhole the second side, then finish off by taking two or three threads across the end and buttonholing over them.

For vertical buttonholes, finish both ends with buttonholed bars.

Buttons

To attach shank-less buttons, first mark their positions. Place the closure together – buttonhole on top – and insert a pin through the centre of the buttonhole to the fabric below. Secure the thread to the right side of the fabric at the place marked.

Slip the button over the needle, place a pin on the button between the holes and work several stitches over it. Remove the pin: wind the thread a few times around the stitches, underneath the button, and fasten off, stitching into the thread shank you have created.

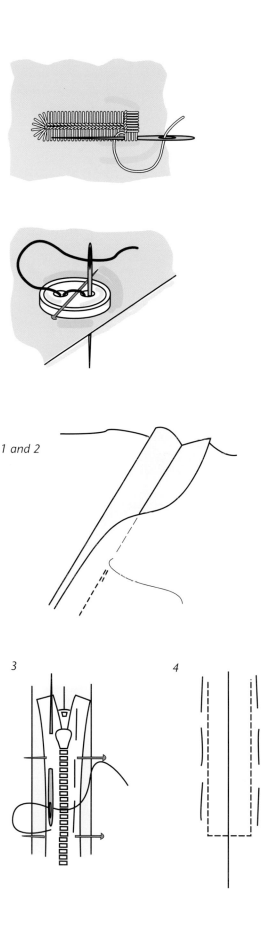

1 and 2

3   4

INSERTING A ZIP

The easiest method of inserting a zip in a cushion cover, where it will not be seen, is the slot seam application, where it is placed in a seam that continues at both ends of the opening.

1 Mark the opening, which should be 1cm (3/8in) longer than the zip teeth. Begin by stitching the seam up to the opening on both sides, reversing a few stitches to secure the ends of the seams.

2 Either machine tack or hand tack the opening edges together, stitching along the seamline. Press the whole seam open, and neaten the raw edges as appropriate.

3 Position the zip face down over the opening seam allowances, with the teeth centred on the seamline. With the bottom stop placed 3mm (1/8in) from the start of the tacking and the pull tab turned upwards, pin and tack through all layers, 5mm (3/16in) from the teeth on either side.

4 Working from the right side and using a zipper foot, stitch around 5mm (3/16in) from the seamline, pivoting the stitching at the corners. Neaten the threads on the wrong side, and remove the tacking stitches to finish.

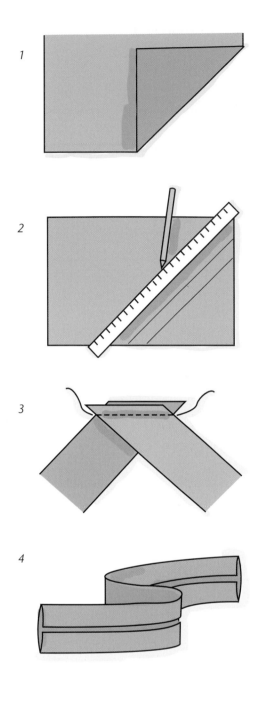

BOUND EDGES

This type of hem is often used to neaten neck and sleeve edges on children's garments, where it gives a neat and decorative finish. For curved edges, it is best to cut the binding on the bias grain, to ensure that it will curve easily and lie flat.

1 Cut bias strips at a 45 degree angle to the selvedge. Fold the crossways edge of the fabric level with the selvedge, press the fold and open out the fabric.

2 Using a ruler and coloured pencil, mark lines parallel to the fold; make each marked strip four times the width that you want your finished binding. Mark and cut out more strips to make up the required length.

3 If necessary, join strips with narrow seams on the straight grain, as shown in the diagram. Trim and press the seam open.

4 Fold the binding lengthways in half, wrong sides together, then fold under the edges so that they almost touch in the middle.

5 Seam allowances on the edges which are to be bound are not needed and should be trimmed off. Open out the binding and cut the ends straight. Fold under the first end by 5mm (^{3}/16in), and place it on the edge of the fabric, right sides facing and edges even.

Start at a place where the join will not show, such as an under arm seam. Pin and tack the binding in place, and with the end unfolded, overlap the fold at the beginning. Machine stitch taking 6mm (^{1}/4in) seams.

6 Press the binding towards the edge. Fold it to the wrong side and slipstitch it over the line of machine sewing. If you prefer the stitching to show, tack instead of slipstitching and topstitch the binding from the right side. Remove the tacking stitches.

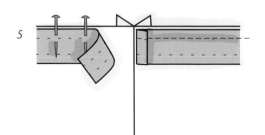

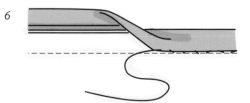

DRAWSTRING

This is a very quick and easy way to close a gathered top, such as the one on the laundry bag, using twisted cord threaded through a channel made in the seam. Alternatively, as with the baby's drawstring bag, you can use ribbon, threaded through a separate band applied to the wrong side.

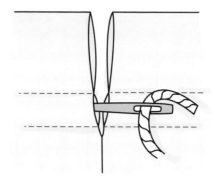

Cut the cord or ribbon into two equal lengths, each measuring twice the length of the channel plus about 50cm (20in) for the hanging loop. Using a ribbon threader or a large safety pin, thread each length through both channels, starting and finishing at opposite sides.

Knot the ends of the cord to secure.

TRANSFERRING MOTIFS

Dressmaker's carbon paper is a quick and reliable technique for transferring embroidery motifs to fabrics with a smooth surface. If you are working on a dark fabric, choose a light-coloured carbon paper such as yellow or white, but for other coloured fabrics, a close tone such as mid-blue or red is generally better.

Begin by tracing the motif with an HB pencil, and transfer any registration marks. Place the fabric on a flat working surface and pin the motif to the right side, registration marks matching. Slip the carbon paper under the tracing, shiny side down; avoid pinning through the carbon paper.

Carefully go over the outlines using an H pencil. Lift a corner of the carbon to check that the line is clear. If not, replace the carbon and go over it again.

INDEX